To Eric
with Best Wishes

Jan and Betty Ann

Christmas 1987.

Relief Woodcarving
and Lettering

Relief Woodcarving
and Lettering

Ian Norbury

STOBART & SON LTD
LONDON

British Library Cataloguing in Publication Data
Norbury, Ian
    Relief woodcarving & lettering.
    1.   Wood-carving — Technique
    I.   Title
736'.4   NK9704

ISBN 0–85442–035–5

Published December 1987 by
Stobart & Son Ltd., 67–73 Worship Street, London EC2A 2EL

Typeset in Garamond by Photo·graphics, Honiton, Devon.
Printed by A. Wheaton & Co. Ltd., Exeter, Devon.

For my wife

By the same author:
Techniques of Creative Woodcarving
Projects for Creative Woodcarving

Contents

Introduction

Over the past year I have found a whole new world of creative possibilities opened up to me which I had previously ignored. The potential for self-expression in relief carving is obvious, yet came to me as a surprise, and I hope that many others will be fascinated by it.

When I started this book I was not terribly enthusiastic, mainly because, like most people, I looked upon relief carving as a lesser art; mostly decorative, often trivial and seldom "important". It did not stand alone as a three dimensional carving does, but was usually part of something else – furniture, architecture, church woodwork, etc.

I therefore set myself two goals: firstly, that I would not put in the book the general principles of work which could be learned from many other books still in print, thereby eliminating most of the traditional decorative stuff, and secondly, what I included would be mainly my current work and hopefully to the taste of the woodcarver who reads my books. That basically excludes the *avant-garde* art student and the dyed-in-the-wool traditionalist.

My criteria for judging what was suitable was simple. As a professional carver with all the usual committments of wife, kids, house, etc., I cannot afford to produce carvings which don't sell. It seems reasonable to me that if somebody wants to buy a carving then there are a few people around who would like to carve something similar. Conversely, if a carving is unsaleable, it's probably a pretty boring carving. Now that

is not an insult to everyone who couldn't sell a carving, it simply means that the mass of people have a range of tastes which fall within certain limits. Much of my work happens to be inside those limits, and sells. Most woodcarvers fall within them also; to those people my books are directed – go beyond those limits and there is a distinct shortage of buyers and readers. So the budding Henry Moores are reading the wrong book.

I found relief carving difficult, more so than in the round, because there is no definite shape. If you carve a three dimensional head, it is either the same shape as the real one or not. But with a relief it doesn't try to be the same, only to *look* the same, and that makes it a matter of personal judgement, not measurement.

As I worked my way up from the simplest subjects to more complex ones I began to realise the possibilities of relief carving. The first that struck me was that suddenly timber was not a problem anymore. No more sitting on large lumps of wood for years on end, waiting for it to dry, and probably crack. Boards up to 75 mm (3″) thick and of a good width, dry and flawless, are available in almost any timber you care to name. This enables you to utilise the full potential of colour, grain, texture and character of those different timbers which, for three dimensional carving, were always too small.

Secondly, the creative opportunities afforded by the pictorial nature of relief came home to me at quite a late stage. That may seem strange, but if you look round at a few churches, museums, books of sculpture, and so on, the pictorial use of relief drowns you. Endless processions of chariots going to Calvary; flights of angels, dozens of cupids, Greek friezes, Roman friezes, Renaissance altar pieces, etc., etc., all in beautifully carved landscapes with superb carved buildings, wash over you until you feel that even if you wanted to carve a relief it could only be a pale shadow of the miracles produced in the past.

I think only by the practice of relief carving, and determinedly doing your own thing, do you come to realise that by using relief, carving which in three dimensions you would have quailed before attempting, you can now accomplish. For example, it is no small thing to carve a horse in the round; a racehorse and jockey running is pretty daunting, but two or three running together is a monumental operation. In relief you can tackle it. Wood is not a problem. The enormous amount of research and knowledge required for the three dimensional carving can be reduced to a little clarification of details. The workload of removing wood is far less; breakage is unlikely and technique is generally easier. Most importantly, you can devote your energies to your own interpretation and expression of the speeding animal – thundering towards you, the track tapering away behind, the distant landscape – whatever you want.

Having said that, it must be pointed out that relief carving is not easy. The difficulties are discussed later in the book but it should be made clear at this point that it is a decision making process, far more than is the case in three dimensional sculpture. Relief is essentially a distortion of nature, and it is for the carver to decide the way the distortions should be made. For this reason the book is less specific in its instructions than are my previous ones. Whereas, when carving a head in the round, I could say this is the precise shape of the nose or chin and this is how to carve it, with relief I can only say that the features on this actual person looked like this, and this is how I have attempted to create an illusion of the real thing within the thickness of the wood I have available. Others may do it differently. To help illustrate the shapes I have made I have included cross sections, which will, I hope, go a long way to helping the reader understand the principles involved.

The carvings pictured are not particularly for copying but as a record of how I have approached the subject and found it increasingly interesting and at times very exciting. I like to think that others might follow the same path, adapting the subjects I have chosen to those of their own, and benefitting from my mistakes and successes.

The lettering section is not as involved as one might expect. Once again, one can carve the traditional lettering, Roman, Gothic, Old English, etc., if that is what you want; but lettering has always been regarded as an art form and I have tried to show that it can be used not only to convey information, but as decoration on sculptures, furniture, buildings etc., or as an end in itself. There are many examples of decoration that are merely there to catch the light and relieve a plain surface. How much better if decoration has some significance, and letters always signify something in one's mind, even if we do not understand the words? One could get very involved in letter carving, and although it perhaps takes a particular type of person to do it very well, it presents no difficulties for the average carver.

CHAPTER ONE

Definition

Whilst, theoretically, I suppose, anything can be carved in relief, a quick study of the work of other sculptors will reveal that certain conventions are generally adhered to. To take an obvious example, you will almost never see a medallion or coin on which the portrait is not in profile. There are a few exceptions and they are fairly successful, but the majority are only a side view of head or head and shoulders. Why is this? Perhaps one's immediate conclusion is that the nose would not flatten down and still look good. However, if we consider a 10p coin (Fig. 1)

Fig. 1

there is perhaps $\frac{1}{2}$mm of relief. Proportionally, the nose is probably about its natural thickness, as is the ear and the coronet. In contrast, however, the shoulder has been reduced from half the width of a body, say 250mm (10″), to the same thickness of the nose, but still looks perfectly convincing; so it is not the nose. I think it is simply a question of what *looks* good.

Looking at the coin again, notice that the profile of the face is outlined against the background, clearly showing the recognisable features of the Queen. (As a front view this outline would merely show her hair and very little of her coronet.) The side view of the eye and the edge of the hair is then outlined against the plain surface of the face, then the coronet against the hair. Next, the shoulder, which you will notice has been brought well forward, cuts across the background and overlays the neck. The top of the dress then lies on top of the shoulders. In smaller detail there are the overlapping waves of the hair; the corner of the mouth sunk into the cheek; the ear laid over the neck, and the nostril over the nose.

These simple devices enable the artist to give an illusion of depth fairly easily, rather in the same way that a drawing of a receding line of telegraph poles will give an illusion

Fig. 2 'Colonel Blood' carved for H.M.Government for the Tower of London

Fig. 3 'Brendan' Courtesy of Mr and Mrs R Gilbert

of perspective and distance. From the front, not only are most of these overlaps missing, but the shapes of the eyes, lips and nose are more subtle, less distinct. Two portraits, 'Colonel Blood' and 'Brendan' are illustrated in figs. 2 and 3, to show further examples of such work.

The same is true of other parts of the body. A foot seen from the front is far less immediately recognisable than from the side. This does not mean that you *cannot* do it, or that you are taking the easy way out, rather that you are doing all you can in order to create a *successful* illusion. I think the only way that rules governing these problems can be learnt is by the study of great sculpture of the past and by actually doing it yourself.

Be prepared for many failures, small successes and the odd wholly successful piece. The important thing is to discover why you have failed and then improve, and to know

why you have succeeded and build on it. Further details about design will be given in the projects.

*   *   *

A relief carving is essentially a modelled shape which is raised above a flat surface. For the purpose of clarity I will refer to the main features of the carving, the figures, flowers or whatever, as the subject, and to the surface from which they are raised as the background. The background may be a wall, as in the case of the carved garlands and swags of Grinling Gibbons; a turned column or vase; a separate board of wood or, more commonly, the actual block of wood from which the subject is carved. There may, in fact, be no background at all, as in the case of a pierced carved screen where the background is the open space seen through the holes.

In cases where the whole piece is carved from a solid panel of wood, the basic principle that the subject is raised above the background means that the background must be lowered around the subject.

Having traced the subject onto the panel it must be very firmly held down. Removing the bulk of the background is known as "wasting" and is a mechanical, sometimes boring task. There are four ways of doing it. Firstly, you can cut round the edge of the design with chisels and cut away the waste up to the line. This although it may seem an obvious thing to do, is not a good idea. When forcing a chisel deeply into the surface of the wood, enormous side pressure is exerted by the thickness of the metal as it drives itself like a wedge, into the fibres. Immediately, damage has been done to your carving. By the second method, a deep vee, or gouge cut is made, 5–6 mm ($\frac{1}{4}$″) outside the line of the subject, then the chisels are stabbed into the line of the drawing, but the side pressure is vented on the thin wall of waste between the line and the vee cut, which crumbles away.

The third method, and I think the best, is to run a vee cut around the design, 5–6 mm ($\frac{1}{4}$″)from the design, and then remove the bulk of the waste with gouges, finally chopping down around the line with chisels and carefully working the background down to meet these cuts. I think this puts the subject least at risk. The fourth way is to use mechanical means such as an electric router, drill press, or other machine, such as in the case of the owl in Figure 62, where I used a circular saw.

The router, as used in the case of Marillion

Figure 181, is favourite today. These are excellent tools in skilled hands, but few of us are very skilled with them. Their advantages are speed, ease, perfect uniformity of depth of cut, the ability to enter small areas of background surrounded by the subject and waste them cleanly and the fact that they leave a perfectly vertical edge to the subject. Plywood templates can be made and followed by the router, permitting it to cut precisely round the exact line of the subject and small cutters are obtainable to enter all but the tightest corners.

The disadvantages, as I see it, are the cost of the machine and cutters, the skill needed to use it and the catastrophes that occur when the skill is lacking. Routers also have limitations which, if one has come to rely on the machine, may inhibit the carver attempting certain types of work. For instance, they cannot really work on a curved surface, convex or concave; they cannot cut a graduated or sloping background such as the form of relief known as tondo, where the background slopes downwards from the edges. However, for many straightforward wasting jobs, machine routers are unbeatable.

Referring back to the third method: when the waste has been removed, the outline of the design must be cut round. This process is called setting-in. It requires finding gouges and chisels to fit the outline exactly and chopping down to the level of the background. This usually requires sharp blows with the mallet. Ensure that the cuts all overlap so that you can be sure the outline is all released from the background before you finish the grounding. The setting-in should be perfectly perpendicular as seen in

Fig. 4 at A. If it is undercut as at B the design will get smaller as the modelling progresses. If the cuts slope outwards as at C, the design will get larger. This is, of course, the lesser of the two evils, so if in doubt slope your cuts outward slightly.

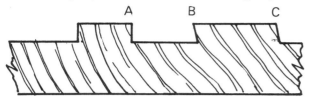

Fig. 4

One of the greatest dangers in setting-in is making cuts away from the line of the design which then leave tool cuts in the background. These are very unsightly and can only be removed by lowering the entire background. The other danger is from insufficient outlining with the vee tool in the first stage. This raises a problem which is fundamental to all woodcarving. The cutting edge of a chisel or gouge is a wedge. When it is pressed in the wood it exerts pressure on the wood either side of the edge and tries to split it apart Fig. 5A. If the strength of the wood has been reduced on one side of the cut by the vee cut or by modelling, the fibres on that side will crumble away and

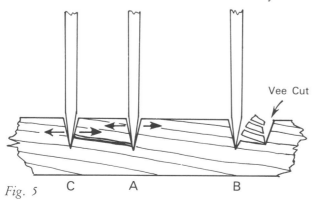

Fig. 5

eliminate the pressure on the other side (Fig. 5B). The design is therefore left intact and undamaged. However, at Fig. 5A, the fibres have actually been slightly moved to either side, and if another cut is made at C a fracture is liable to be caused along the line of the grain between A and C, because of the sideways pressure from the cut at C. In practise this means that when you make a cut where a thin part of the design may be dislodged make sure that the waste is weaker than the design, so that the waste will crumble away rather than the design.

After the setting-in, the background must be given a smooth tooled finish. This is really done in combination with the setting-in, in that the sharp vertical cuts must coincide with a clean horizontal cut across the surface of the background. It is important

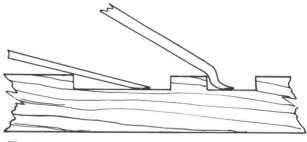

Fig. 6

that the background is lowered to a uniform depth (assuming it is required flat) and this should be measured. All too often there is a tendency to cut less deeply in the more difficult areas. Most of the background can usually be flattened with normal straight gouges of a shallow curve, such as a No. 3 chisel; No. 1's are not suitable as the corners always tend to dig in. In confined areas a grounding tool may be necessary. Grounding tools are similar to spoon bent or front bent gouges but not as curved. They will get in recesses and undercuts where straight tools would dig in (Fig. 6). Ground cuts should be made with the grain as much as possible to leave clean shining tool cuts. Where you must cut against the grain use very sharp tools and try to slice the blade from side to side to get a cleaner cut. Of course, you may want to sand the background or texture it with matting punches and although this is generally regarded as a cover-up for bad grounding, I think it can look effective.

Obviously, wasting, setting-in and grounding on shallow, low relief carvings, removing perhaps, between 6–12 mm ($\frac{1}{4}''$–$\frac{1}{2}''$) of wood, is relatively easy. As the relief becomes higher, it becomes progressively more laborious and difficult. Also with middle and high relief there is more undercutting, so the setting-in and grounding do not end at the vertical cut. This will be dealt with in detail later.

DESIGN

A three-dimensional sculpture is intended to be seen from all sides, Fig. 7A. It can be placed anywhere; the more accessible to the viewer, the better, but this is not normally a consideration in the design. In relief carving the situation is different. Firstly, because relief carvings are distorted or flattened to varying extents, they must be viewed from a limited number of positions, decreasing as the relief becomes lower. The illusion of depth and perspective only works properly from the viewpoint it was designed for. Fig. 7B.

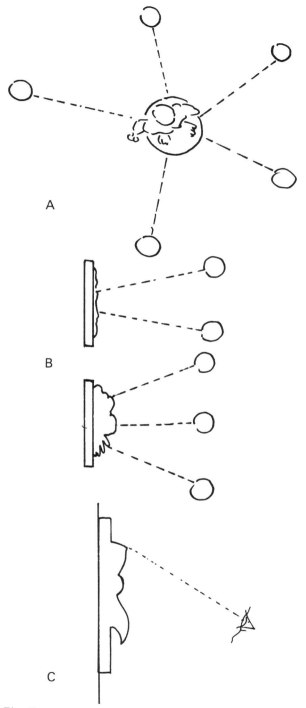

Fig. 7

Fig. 8a

Fig. 8b

This applies not only horizontally but vertically. For instance, a portrait relief designed to be hung three metres (ten feet) above the ground will be undercut around the lower edges but not around the upper ones. Fig. 7C. It may be designed to lean outwards slightly so that it is at right angles to the viewer's line of sight. Viewpoint, then, to some extent, must be taken into account. The above photographs of an old panel, Figures 8a and 8b, further illustrate the differences in viewing angle

Perhaps equally important is function or presentation. For example, if a low relief panel is to fit in a door frame it must be completely clear of the edges to fit into the groove or rebate. The panel of Marillion, Fig. 94, for instance, has its own frame cut from the block. It could be inserted in a door frame, picture frame, or similar setting. The still life, Fig. 52, however, seen from the side, could not fit into any normal frame. It would have to be as deep as the deepest part of the panel, with no rebate. You have to ask yourself what you are going to do with the carving when it is finished. A good example is the nude, Fig. 9 and 10, right. Seen in this photograph it looks fine. However, looked at in its entirety it has a little "platform" of ground standing out from the front. It cannot really go in a frame. If it is fixed on the wall, the platform is just left hanging in mid-air. It can only stand there on a flat surface looking rather homeless, where, from nearly every viewing angle, you can see the edges, the top or the back of the panel. This is lack of forethought and bad design. Had it been hollowed out of a block, the platform would have become part of the sloping background, and the panel could have been framed or mounted in some way. Fig. 11, right.

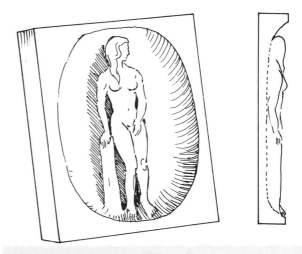

Fig. 9

Fig. 10

GRAIN

The grain of the wood has greater significance in relief carving than it does when carving in the round. Producing the clean curves of the stylised leaf or sharp lines with a vee tool necessitates understanding and an allowance for the fibrous structure of the wood. Failure in this respect will result in chipped corners and torn edges.

Fig. 12 shows a panel of wood with the "grain" or fibres running along its length. The cut A–B is termed "with the grain"; that is to say it is running generally in the direction of the fibres. "Across the grain" refers to cuts at right angles to, or obliquely across the fibres, as in C–D and E–F. Many woods have alternate bands of hard and soft grain and these will tend to cause a cut such as A–B to deviate from the straight line because the tool will try to follow a softer line of grain. With practise it will be found that the harder lines of grain can be allowed for and complete control of the tool achieved. The chips from the cuts along the grain do not break off and the tool must be brought to the surface to release them, or they must be cut off with a knife of skew chisel. The tool will cut across the grain, C–D, in a far more controlled way; the nearer to right angles the better. Also the chips break off whenever the tool is stopped. The oblique cut E–F causes more problems. It will be seen that if we make this cut with a vee tool the right-hand side of the cut will be clean and shiny while the left-hand side is not, and may, in fact, be rough and torn. If the cut G–H is made the opposite situation will occur, i.e. the left-hand side will be clean and the right-hand side will be rough. This clean side is the one that we want nearest to the line of our design. To achieve

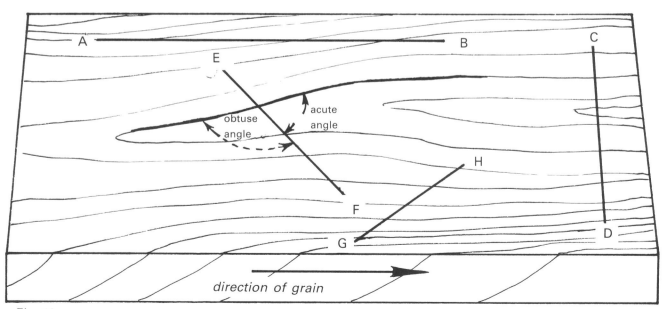

Fig. 12

this, the rules governing the behaviour of the grain must be understood. Observe that the clean side of the cut always meets the fibres of the wood at an acute angle, whereas the rough side meets it at an obtuse angle. The side that is clean is running "with the grain"; the rough side is running "against the grain". In other words the tool cuts cleanly when it is cutting *away* from the ends of the fibres and cuts roughly when it is cutting *into* the ends of the fibres. Another way of putting it, is that when we cut from a shorter fibre to a longer fibre we are cutting "with the grain" and cutting cleanly. When the cut is from a longer fibre to a shorter one we are cutting "against the grain" and not cutting cleanly. A simple trial of the procedure will demonstrate clearly what is very difficult to explain in words.

Experience will show you that the degree of "graininess" of woods varies considerably; some will simply not tolerate being cut against the grain and the tool will bury itself in the wood. Others, such as lime are very kind and, given razor sharp tools, seem to be almost grainless. Of course, it follows that the grain in the thickness of the wood must also be taken into account. This can be seen on the edge of the length of the panel. If the board has been cut in such a way that the grain is running at an angle across the thickness, as in Fig. 12, it will be easy to cut in the direction shown, but very difficult to cut in the opposite direction. Although it is wise to select panels which have straight grain running parallel to the surface, this must always be taken into account to a greater or lesser extent.

TOOLS AND EQUIPMENT

The range of tools required for carving has been discussed at length in every book on the subject including my own *Techniques of Creative Woodcarving*, and I would refer readers to it for a detailed description of the use and maintenance of woodcarving equipment. The gouges and chisels used in relief carving are essentially the same as those for carving in the round, but with more accent on spoon bent tools and less on the larger half round ones used for roughing out. On a relief, one is not generally cutting very deeply so these larger gouges are not so useful. Recessing the background and undercutting are much more in evidence.

It is difficult to specify a range of gouges, since they are, to a large extent, dictated by the precise type and scale of the work undertaken. However, in principle, the general requirement is as follows: setting-in the outline of the relief on the panel usually requires a vee tool, the size obviously dependent on the size of carving. Roughing out the background will be done with a half round gouge. The relief is then cut in accurately with a variety of shallower gouges which must closely follow the design line. The background must then be flattened and tooled to a smooth surface using flat gouges Nos. 2 and 3 and probably some spoon bent tools of the same shape. Flat chisels (No. 1's) are rarely used for this since the corners tend to dig in.

The modelling and detailing again requires a wide variety of shapes and sizes. It should be clear that until you have acquired a fairly wide range of gouges, perhaps 20 or 30, the range of sizes on which you can work will be limited. I think it is probably best to bear in mind the scale when buying tools and initially confine your work to a certain size range. This is not as inhibiting as it might seem, however it is reasonable to say that you cannot carve a portrait medallion 75mm (3″) across with the same set of tools as a 300mm (12″) square panel, although their use is not excluded. Below I have included a list of gouges that I feel would encompass the average range of work undertaken by a beginner.

Apart from chisels and gouges you will need a mallet, bench and holding devices, G-cramps, bench vice, holdfast, etc. One or two knives with long thin points will be found invaluable for cutting cleanly into tight corners. Rifler files are used for cleaning up in awkward hollows and corners and, of course, abrasives as needed. A machine using rotary burrs, whether of the flexibile shafted or hand-held type can be very useful for making small recesses and holes. Indeed, extensive amounts, and even the whole of a carving, are carried out with them by some people. An electric router can remove backgrounds quickly and efficiently although considerable skill is required in handling it to achieve the maximum benefit.

Sharpening is, of course, of paramount importance. I discussed this in *Techniques of Creative Woodcarving* and will only mention now that I have changed my sharpening machine slightly. I now use a disc with a fine self-adhesive sanding disc on it to produce the edge, followed by "stropping" on a felt wheel dressed with polishing paste. I find this produces a superlative edge without any rounding of the bevel, which

may be experienced using only continual stropping. Also, make sure you have a few slip stones for small gouges and vee tools.

Regarding timber, unlike three dimensional carving, you are not as limited by the dimensions of wood available when carving reliefs. Boards of almost any timber are available today and you can experiment and explore to your heart's content. However, limewood is the easy option, being cheap and very easy to carve. My own favourite is probably English walnut, but I try anything.

Gouges (Swiss tool numbers shown)

No.12 (vee tool)	8mm $\left(\frac{5}{16}''\right)$
	2mm $\left(\frac{3}{32}''\right)$
No.9 (gouge)	13mm $\left(\frac{1}{2}''\right)$
No.7 (gouge)	14mm $\left(\frac{9}{16}''\right)$
No.3 (gouge)	12mm $\left(\frac{7}{16}''\right)$
	5mm $\left(\frac{3}{16}''\right)$
No.1s (skew)	5mm $\left(\frac{3}{16}''\right)$
No.2a (spoonbent)	8mm $\left(\frac{5}{16}''\right)$
	2mm $\left(\frac{3}{32}''\right)$
No.11 (gouge)	3mm $\left(\frac{1}{8}''\right)$
	1mm $\left(\frac{3}{64}''\right)$
No. 8 (gouge)	4mm $\left(\frac{5}{32}''\right)$
No.2 (gouge)	8mm $\left(\frac{5}{16}''\right)$
	2mm $\left(\frac{3}{32}''\right)$
No.3F (fish tail) (for serifs)	8mm $\left(\frac{5}{16}''\right)$

Note: English and Swiss tool numbers differ.

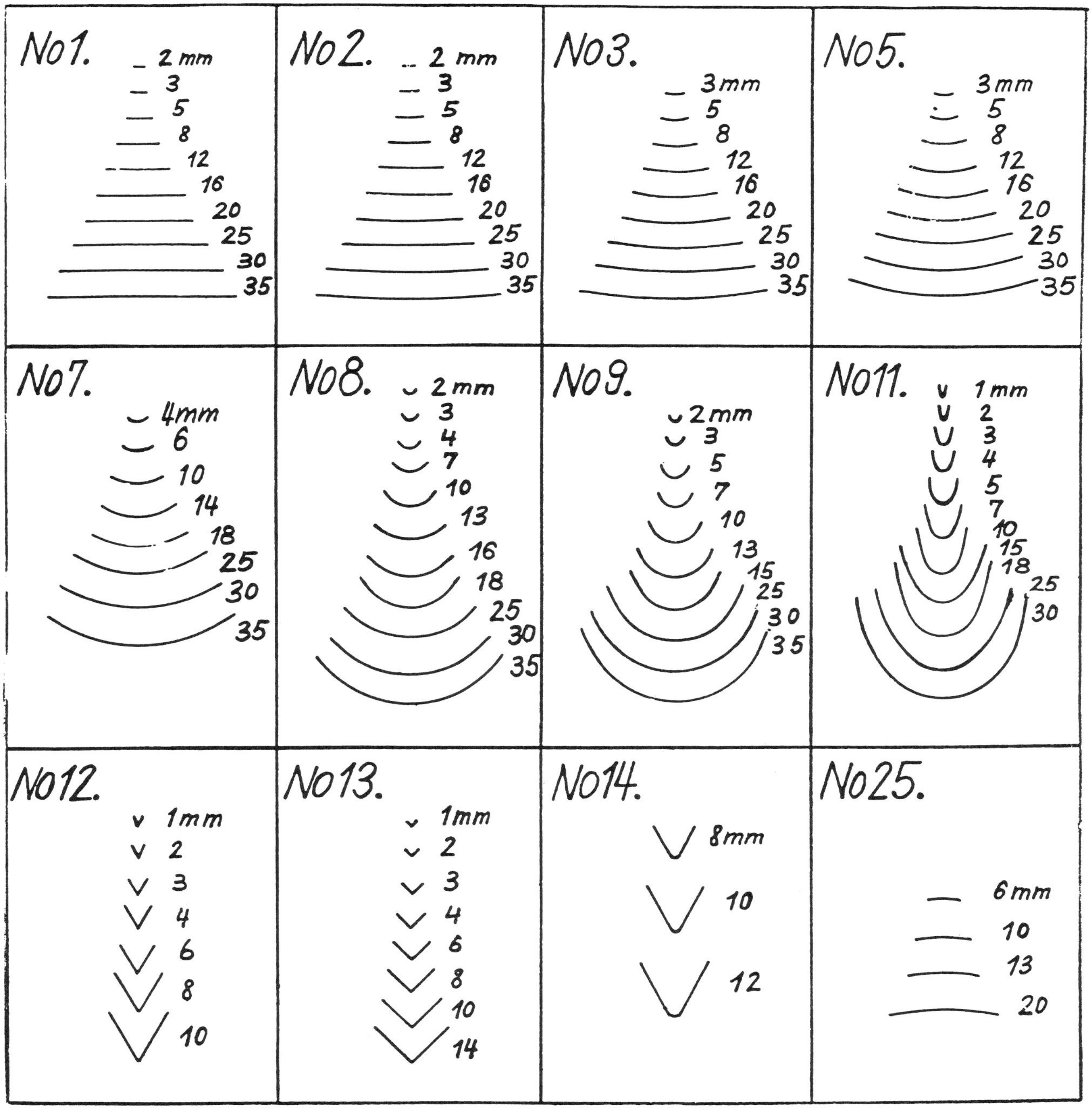

Fig. 13 Tool shape diagram (Swiss Numbering)

CHAPTER TWO

The Vee Tool

The vee tool, which performs basically the same job as the engraver's burin, is a very useful implement, but often abused by being made to do work it is not really suited to. For instance, it will often be seen used to shown the veins on leaves, or the divisions between the fingers on a hand. These are not vee shaped but rounded and curved, and the use of the vee tool leaves them with an unnatural linear appearance. The best use for a vee tool is to make lines, although it is also very good for cutting and cleaning up corners. Given a good sharp tool, in practised hands it can be used almost like a writing instrument.

Of course the principles laid out in the section on grain are absolutely true for the vee tool, but there are plenty of timbers which allow it to cut in any direction very cleanly. Getting it really sharp is always a problem. If, when sharpened, it is treated as two flat chisels joined together, a small beak will appear at the point of the vee. This can then be carefully removed using a small oilstone. However, if the tool is sharpened as if it were a very small gouge with high straight sides, the beak will not appear.

To sharpen, lay the tool on one side on the stone and after a few strokes begin to roll it over the vee, still honing, onto the other side. When the honing is completed the burr must be removed from the inside with a small slipstone of appropriate shape. This must be done delicately and sensitively, not just given a quick rub, otherwise wavy or scalloped edges will result. Only use will determine when the tool is sharp; the clean, whistling sound it makes slicing across a piece of softwood is quite unmistakable.

STRAIGHT LINE WORK – CHURCH DESIGN

The first subject provides the basis for good practice with the vee tool and has been chosen for its straight lines; (curves are undoubtedly more difficult with this tool). The drawing was taken from a small tourist guide and could be enlarged by the usual method of drawing grids, or more easily by the use of the enlarging facility on a photocopier. The wood used here was English field maple, a tough hardwood, but fine grained and clean cutting. It was sanded to a fine, smooth surface and the drawing traced onto it.

Now, with the board held down firmly in a bench vice or on the bench top with clamps or screws, work can begin.

Obviously, it is best to have the surface clear of obstructions such as holdfasts and G-cramps whenever possible. The tool should be held in both hands, one on the handle pushing, and the other at the top of the blade pulling back. With it balanced between these two opposing forces, great control can be achieved. Fig. 14.

Whilst there is no special reason to start at a particular point in the design, it is logical to outline the basic shapes of the picture and then fill in the details. One practical advantage would be to plan your cuts so that one runs into the side of a previous one if possible; for instance, if you are making a "T", you would make the top stroke first and then cut the upright to run into it, rather than cutting the upright and having

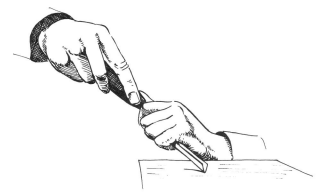

Fig. 14

to judge the exact position of the cross stroke to coincide with the top of the upright. Many cuts along the grain will have to be knicked off with a knife or skew chisel.

It is very important that there be some variation in the thickness of the lines. Uni-

CLAPTON CHURCH.

Fig. 15

form, even lines will be dull and lifeless. Look at examples of pen drawings, charcoal sketches, etc., and you will see the artist's sensitive use of line to give stress and vitality to a design.

When the carving is finished, it is lightly sanded with fine paper to remove any trace of the drawing.

The carving illustrated (Fig. 15) was given two coats of shellac sealer, the liquid being allowed to settle in the vee cuts. When perfectly dry it was sanded again to remove the sealer from the flat surface and wax polished. That left the vee cuts a darker brown against the white of the plain areas.

Although this is probably the simplest form of carving I can imagine, and is, I suppose, strictly speaking, engraving, it creates a pleasing object and is a satisfying and useful introduction to the craft.

Examples can be seen on antique furniture and other objects from all periods. The principle could be expanded and exploited in various ways: the wood could be stained dark or painted and the dark surface cut through to create a white line effect. Conversely, the cuts could be painted, stained or even filled with a coloured material such as resin. It can be used on furniture, mouldings, turnings and so on. Personally, I think that portraits of houses and churches cut into beautiful pieces of wood could form a very commercial product.

CURVED LINE WORK – LION

It is far more difficult to produce good curves with a vee tool and the design shown in Fig. 16 will help the beginner gain good

Fig. 16 Curved line work — Lion (Courtesy of Mr and Mrs G. Dawes)

control with such work.

Assuming that the drawing has been transferred to the wood, start with the main lines such as the spine, tail and legs. The tool must start on the surface of the wood and slide down into it so that the cut has a tapering end. Similarly, at the end of the cut the tool must be brought up out of the wood to give the same effect. Also, in curves, variation of thickness is even more important to give a fluid, lively line. It is difficult to follow a curved line exactly without it having a dead, copied look, rather like the difference between a freehand drawing and a tracing. It is better, therefore, to sacrifice accuracy to the spontaneity and fluidity of the curve; in other words, start with a good sweep of the tool; if it wanders from the line, don't jerk it back and spoil the curve, but continue with the sweep. It may not be perfectly accurate but it will look better.

Fig. 17

Obviously, a straight bladed tool cannot cut a curve without its side pressing hard into the outside edge of the curve. This is not noticeable until very small radii are attempted. Then it will be found that the outer edge of the cut gets crushed and the cut itself is rough and broken as the tool jerks round the bend. It will then be necessary to cut the curve with a small gouge of appropriate sweep, imitating the vee cut by two cuts of the gouge. This is the case on the lion's claws and toes (Fig. 17).

ADVANCED VEE TOOL WORK – STANDING CUP

The precise function of standing cups is not known. It has been suggested that they were elaborate communion vessels, but wooden communion cups were in fact banned by the canons of Winchester in 1071 long before standing cups were made. Edward H. Pinto, author of *Treen and Other Wooden Bygones* believed they formed part of the insignia of some exclusive 17th century society. They all date from that period and the majority carry the royal coat of arms and illustrations of animals which represent aristocratic families.

Whatever their purpose they are normally 350–500mm (14″–20″) high and 125–250mm (5″–10″) in diameter made of pear, cherry, maple or sycamore. They consist of a base, stem, bowl with lid and knob which usually is hollowed to form a spice cup, also with lid. The turning is very fine in the earlier specimens but become rather heavier later. The engraving on the surface is extremely fine and complex. Apart from copious amounts of purely decorative work there are coats of arms, birds, animals, foliage and invariably bands of religious text of considerable length. (See Fig. 156 in lettering examples.) It is debateable whether these designs were in fact carved with a cutting tool or burnt with a hot steel scriber, in a similar way to modern pyrography. However it seems to me that, certainly on some of them, the lines are cut very deeply for pyrography. Be that as it may, the decorations are in the form of etched lines which are blackened, whether by stain or heat.

The cup illustrated, Fig. 18, was commissioned by the organiser of a series of exhibitions related to the Arthurian legends of which the Grail Cup forms an essential element. It was to stand on a decorative wrought iron pedestal in the centre of the Round Table. The decorations were to relate to the legends but were not to be of the quasi-religious mystical nonsense that is so often found associated with them.

The final result has original designs taken from 17th century standing cups as a basis, with small armorial devices and symbols added.

On the spice cup are a lion and a dove, Fig. 19. The lid has only stylised foliage motifs. The cup has on one side a representation of the dove of heaven descending into the Grail, taken from a Byzantine stone carving, Fig. 20; and on the other side a stag with a crucifix between its antlers, Fig. 22, a common medieval symbol of Christ. Above these illustrations is a band of lettering cut with a vee tool, with a little occasional help from a small gouge. The words are "LUMIN ULTRA LUMENS" which apparently mean "light beyond light" a quotation referring to the Grail. (See also the chapter on lettering). The stem, Fig. 21, is carved with abstract patterns and foliage, whilst the base bears the supposed coats of arms of Galahad,

Fig. 18   By courtesy of Mr. I. Robertson

Fig. 19

Fig. 20

Fig. 21

Fig. 22

Percival and Bors, the only knights of the Round Table to succeed in finding the Grail. Between the three shields are five petalled roses, ancient symbols of peace.

A golden coloured wood seemed appropriate for this work and pear, being a traditional material for standing cups, made its use an easy choice. It was finished with amber french polish to enhance its pinky-yellow colour.

The turning is simple enough (Fig. 23) and the parts can be held in a bench vice or screwed to a waste block for the carving, all of which was carried out with a small vee tool, except for chipping out the odd corner with a knife tip. Pear is absolutely ideal for this kind of work, cutting very cleanly without being too hard.

When the carving is finished, brush on a coat of brown sealer, leave to dry and sand off with 300 grit paper. Repeat several times until you feel the engraved lines are dark enough; in my case, four coats. After the final rub down, give two coats of amber french polish, leave to harden and polish with fine steel wool and wax.

This type of decoration is so simple to do and so immediate in its execution that I feel there is great potential here for the carver, especially the beginner, who could use it on all manner of objects with the absolute minimum of equipment and experience. On the other hand, the skilled cabinet maker, turner or carpenter might well find it adaptable in its more sophisticated forms.

Fig. 23

INTRODUCTION TO EGYPTIAN RELIEF – PISCES

The next advance from the simple vee cut is to introduce a small amount of modelling. The technique, sometimes known as Egyptian relief carving from its common use in the ancient buildings of that country, consists simply of making a deep vee cut round the outline of the design and then rounding off the inside edge. This produces a very low relief carving which appears to be inlaid into the block of wood. (Fig. 24). The modelling

Fig. 24

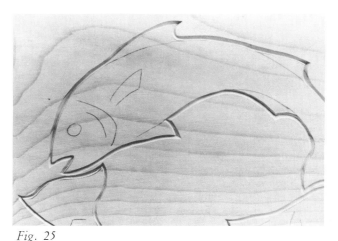

Fig. 25

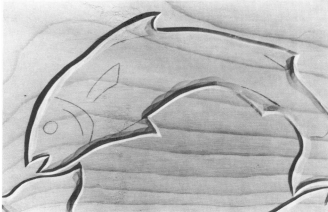

Fig. 26

is very simple and only one or two shallow gouges are needed. Figs. 25 and 26. Some details in the design will also be cut in the same way. Fig. 27.

I used cedar of Lebanon which does not cut very well with the vee tool and great care must be taken not to split the wood when cutting against the grain. One way round this problem is to make the cut one way to produce one clean edge and then cut back the other way, shaving down the torn edge and missing the clean edge. The edge is cut in with a gouge and most of the corners are finished with a knife. The carving can be carefully sanded and waxed polished. Cedar takes a beautiful, silky finish and has a bold grain pattern, but I would not recommend it for fine work.

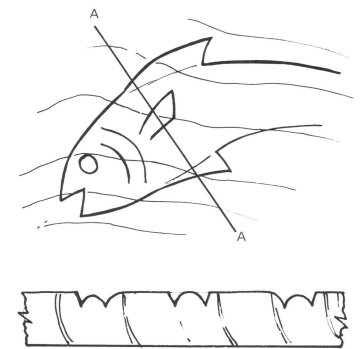

Fig. 27

ADVANCED EGYPTIAN RELIEF – TUTANKHAMUN PANEL

When the tomb of the boy-king Tutankhamun was opened in 1922, the world was astonished at the beauty and craftsmanship of the contents. Egyptian art, previously much admired, soared to new heights. This was, after all, the first important tomb to be discovered which had not been virtually emptied before. As much as I personally deplore grave robbing, one cannot but marvel at its result. It is a whole field of art which is relatively unexplored except by archaeologists. The woodwork, furniture

Fig. 28

and carving is superb. This is not the primitive chippings of a dark age community, but the sophisticated product of a civilisation already some 3,000 years old when Tutankhamun was born. As the archaeologist Flinders Petrie said in his *History of Egypt* "They are unique in their splendid power, which no self-conscious civilisation has ever rivalled, nor can hope to rival, and in their enduring greatness they may last till all the feebler works of man have perished."

The relief I have copied, shown in Fig. 28, is carved on the end of a cedarwood coffer, now in Cairo Museum. The original design is perhaps 300mm (12″) square. It depicts the god "Onnophris, who is at the head of the West, the great god, lord of the Necropolis", better known as Osiris, facing the dead king who wears a crown, a broad collar and streamers and a kilt. The kilt may look strange, but was in fact starched to project in a great point at the front. He offers the god a lamp and a pot. The god wears a crown with ostrich plumes, an artificial beard strapped to his chin and a long white garment from which his hands protrude, one holding a long crook and the other a flail. Between them is a pedestal on which stands a vase, its spout in the shape of an ostrich feather depicting truth and justice. Above the figures is an inscription in hieroglyphics.

Having only a photograph in a book, I had to draw this out very carefully, taking accurate measurements and enlarging them. Various points became apparent in doing so. For example, the pedestal is exactly central and the centre of the vase is the dead centre of the panel, in alignment with the fingertips of the hand holding the pot and the line between the hieroglyphs. A circle centred on the knob of the vase passes through the pedestal top and the inner elbows of the figure. A larger circle passes through the bottom edge of the inscription and follows the curves down the front of both bodies. A third circle will pass through the top edge of the inscription, the left elbow of Osiris and the corner of the scarf hanging down Tutankhamun's back. Notice also that the eyes are exactly level and in line with the lower edge of the inscription. The elbows are exactly in a horizontal line, and the angles of them and the crook and flail, are very similar, creating a row of triangles. Also the distance from the top of the panel to the bottom of the inscription is exactly equal to that from the inscription to the elbows, and the same is true of the distance from the elbows to the base of the kilt and from there to the lower edge of the panel. Further research into the subject revealed that in all Egyptian relief paintings and carvings the major figures were drawn onto a precise grid eighteen squares high. The horizontal lines of this grid crossed specified parts of the body: for instance, the hairline, the shoulders, the knees, and so on. The parts of the body were of precise lengths – the foot, three squares, the forearm, five squares – and thickness. Combined with a great desire for balance and a highly formalised and stylised symbolism inherent in all their work, it would appear that the panel is probably far more geometrically contrived than it at first appears.

As a carving it has progressed considerably from the previous example. It is, in fact, virtually a low relief without the background

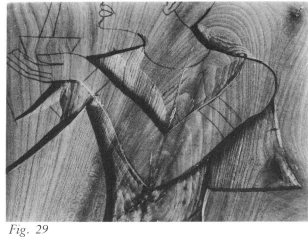

Fig. 29

Fig. 30

Fig. 31

Fig. 32

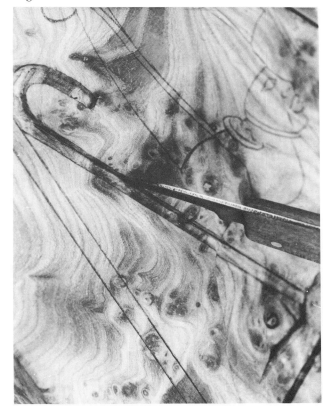

recessed. I can think of no reason why these were done in this way other than the fact that it leaves the wall or surface still effectively flat overall. Of course it involves less work than a normal relief, but labour does not seem to have been a problem in ancient Egypt. Also they were eminently capable of producing raised reliefs and sometimes did.

I have used burr elm, 50mm (2″) thick and 500mm (20″) square, firstly to enhance the carving by the beauty of the wood and secondly to give it a heavy monolithic appearance. The carving is quite simple, indeed it seems to have been designed to be so. Most of the initial cutting is done with a vee tool helped by a knife. Fig. 29 shows the vee tool cuts on the left arm, and the body being recessed with a flat gouge. Fig. 30 shows the head, having been incised, now being modelled, and Fig. 31 shows it almost finished. Cutting in the detail of the crook with a knife is shown in Fig. 32. This is interesting since the lower end of the crook is at surface height, and as it slopes away across the shoulder, so the crook is recessed deeper and deeper into the wood, just as it would in a normal relief carving. Fig. 33 shows the simple treatment of the odd-looking kilt.

The carved areas are left finely tooled whilst the surface is carefully sanded. The hieroglyphs are simply chipped in, without worrying too much about their accuracy. The lettering at the bottom is very straight forward. The techniques are dealt with in Chapter 6, Lettering. They are painted in gold and the final finish is teak oil. (Fig. 34)

I found the whole project quite fascinating and a potential source of much further work.

Fig. 33

Fig. 34 By courtesy of Mr D.C.C. Wilson

CHAPTER THREE

Low Relief

INTRODUCTION TO LOW RELIEF – SHIELD

In all the work so far the overall flat surface of the panel has been maintained and only the subjects have been carved, the background being left untouched. You have produced, in fact, a relief carving which is sunk into the block of wood. To progress further it must be drawn out of the block.

If you produce an Egyptian relief carving and then lower the background to the depth of the vee cuts, you have produced a bas-relief or low relief; that is, you have a design which is very slightly raised up above its background, or matrix.

There is no real definition of a low relief that enables one to differentiate it from a middle relief or mezzo-relief. Some are very shallow indeed; for instance, the head on a coin is a low relief, and in the Victoria and Albert Museum there is a cabinet which has scenes in relief carved within the thickness of ebony veneer.

This simple shield illustrates the principle of low relief. As can be seen from Fig. 35, it consists of a lion's head and the border with fleur-de-lys. This could be simply incised like the previous pieces and left at

that. However, the slight difference here is that the background has an heraldic significance in that it is quartered in two colours, whilst the others had no background at all. Therefore, if the lion's head and border are incised and the background lowered slightly, the quartering can be indicated by delineating the edges of the areas of the colours.

The shield, showing the badge of the Heraldry Society, is traced onto an oak blank which has been planed to a shallow curve. The outlines are carefully cut in with the vee tool to a depth of about 4mm. ($^5/_{32}''$). Considerable use of a knife or skew chisel and one or two small, shallow gouges will be necessary in the corners and tight curves.

When the outline is all incised the background must be lowered. Fig. 36. On a relief this shallow, an ordinary straight gouge can be used, say a 6mm ($\frac{1}{4}''$) No. 3 or No. 2. It must be done with care, paring away the larger areas first and then working up to the edges and corners. (Fig. 37). On a larger scale an electric router might be used, but this is discussed in more detail later.

With the background removed and pared to a finely tooled finish some minor shaping can be done: the shape of the face incised and the edges rounded; the eyes cut in with a gouge, and vee tool cuts made down the centres of the fleur-de-lys and mane. The tongue is incised and the mouth slightly hollowed out. The relief is sanded if required and the background may be punched.

This really marks the limits of the vee tool. There is no real advantage in trying to cut deeper relief with it; it is easier to use the techniques of middle and high relief. However, very sophisticated and complex work can, and has been done, using this method and the next project illustrates this.

Fig. 35

Fig. 36

Fig. 37

LOW RELIEF, ADVANCED WORK – BADGE OF THE ROYAL ENGINEERS

One of the commonest uses for low relief work of the former type is for making moulds. This was particularly true in the past when extensive use was made of decorative castings in plaster, iron, brass, bronze and other materials. Looking at the fine brass nameplates on safes, the mouldings on the ceilings of stately homes or the iron balcony round a bandstand, it is easy to forget that somebody had to make the original, and very often it was a woodcarver. The easiest form of casting metal is in sand. The original carving is pressed into a tray of specially prepared sand and withdrawn to leave a perfect impression of the model. Molten metal is then poured into the impression,

thereby reproducing the original. Although other techniques have replaced this process to a large extent, it is still widely used and there is still a demand for the pattern maker.

The Severn Valley Railway restored a locomotive which was used in Persia by the Royal Engineers in the war. In September 1986 the engine was dedicated to the railwaymen who gave their lives in the war and a bronze commemorative plaque incorporating the badge of the Royal Engineers was fixed to the engine's side. To cast the badge a pattern was needed and I was asked to produce a carving, approximately 90mm (3½″) diameter and 6mm (¼″) thick.

Boxwood is the obvious choice for this

Fig. 38

Fig. 39

Fig. 40

Fig. 41

kind of work since its fine hard grain permits the carving of tiny detail.

To produce the carving the badge is traced onto a suitably sized panel. The outline then cut out and the piece glued to a block of wood, using paper between the two pieces to enable it to be easily removed. Fig. 38 and 39. The entire carving requires only the smallest of chisels to be used, from 6mm ($\frac{1}{4}''$) down.

The first stage was to cut in round the crown, the belt and the scroll, then down the inner edge of the central row of leaves and reduce the area between, this row of leaves being lower. The outside row of leaves was also lowered. Now the overlapping leaves could be cut and the tiny central rib

incised either side with a 1.5mm (1/16″) vee tool. Fig. 40. A small pointed knife was also used to clean the corners. The tiny berries were very difficult and could only be pared to shape with a 1.5mm (1/16″) No. 3. The crown was done next. Fig. 41.

This is not the sort of carving where you make a series of cuts and the shape appears. It consists, rather, of fiddling about with tiny cutting tools of any description in order to remove pieces of wood you can hardly see. Of course, carving on a much smaller scale than this is done, but specialised tools are used.

Most difficult of all, I found, was the lettering because it is so instantly recognisable as being wrong. The out-lines of the letters themselves are cut with small chisels and gouges and the spaces between roughly removed, and then flattened with punches which can be made from nails ground to shape. However, the serifs are really not terribly good – more, triangular lumps on the ends of the letters. Fig. 42.

In order for the pattern to withdraw perfectly from the sand, all the edges of the

Fig. 42 *By courtesy of the Severn Valley Railway.*

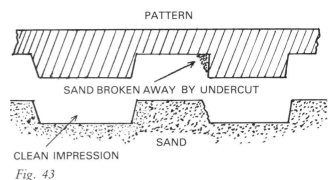

Fig. 43

Fig. 44

carving must slope inwards – there must not only be absolutely no undercutting, but not even vertical edges, otherwise the sand will cling to these edges and break away when the pattern is pulled out. Fig. 43. Bearing this in mind this is not an easy carving and I spent a considerable time sanding, filing and punching the background. Still it came back from the foundry for alterations, and on the finished casting small lumps of sand can be seen where the relief on the uprights was insufficient. However, it is a useful and interesting technique to try since brass and bronze casting is relatively cheap and might well be tried by the amateur craftsman. Fig. 44 shows the bonze casting.

Fig. 45

Fig. 46

Fig. 45 shows an old mould for making plaster flowers. This is incised into the wood rather than carved in relief so that the plaster is pressed into the carving and the finished flower produced in one operation.

Fig. 46 shows another variation, a Japanese rice mould, also cut into the wood. This type of carving is called intaglio.

LOW RELIEF – MODELLING

The carvings up to now have not been "sculptural" in the sense of being shaped or modelled to imitate the form of a real object, but more a cutting of the surface in order to create light and shadow which will convey information visually and, hopefully, in an interesting, decorative or otherwise stimulating manner. Whilst one would not want to imply any artistic or aesthetic value or judgement against the former, there is little doubt that relief carving is seen by most people as a shape raised above the background, carved to give an illustration of reality.

There are few hard and fast principles in relief carving; it is a process that is largely intuitive and therefore difficult to explain.

The following exercise demonstrates some of these difficulties for the beginner and the method of working through the problems as they arise.

CYLINDER, SPHERE AND CUBE

This set up illustrated in Fig. 47, shows a cylinder, sphere and cube on a flat white table. First draw this approximately life size and in true perspective, and then trace this onto a limewood panel. Fig. 48a.

The first stage in carving is to cut in along the top outline and remove the waste wood by hand, or with a router, Fig. 49, to approximately half the depth of the wood, Fig. 48b. Then a series of decisions has to

Fig. 47

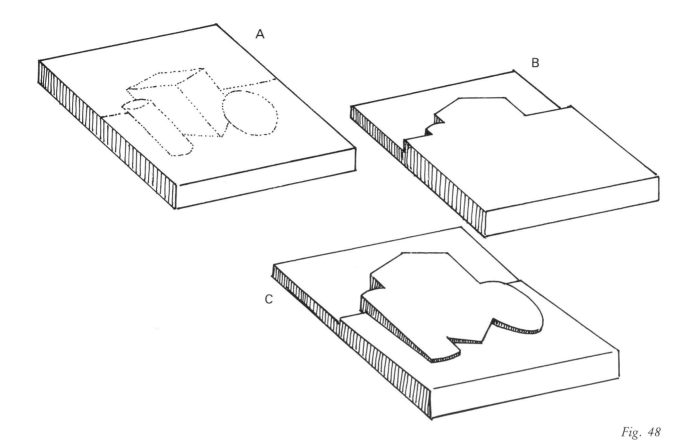

Fig. 48

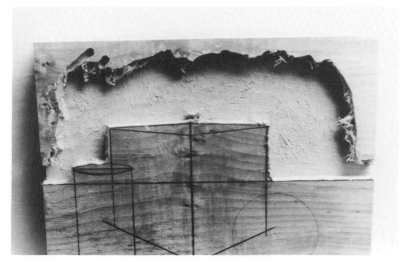

Fig. 49

be made concerning the degree of angle at which the table top and other parts project from the reduced surface of the wood and how they all finally fit together.

In this carving I decided to slope the table top backwards for maximum height at the bottom of the panel, to the minimum height, that is, the back edge of the table halfway up the panel. The difference between the table and background at this point is about 3mm ($\frac{1''}{8}$). This requires setting–in around the cylinder, sphere and the lower half of the cube and carefully sloping the table, leaving the three objects untouched. Fig. 48c.

When I first did this exercise the base edges of the cylinder and cube that should have met the table top were in fact standing away from it about 2mm (3/32"), because I had sloped the table top and had not similarly sloped the cylinder and cube Fig. 50A. Obviously, then, the cylinder and cube must also be sloped downwards, to meet the table top. Fig. 50B.

The cube can now be shaped, angling back from the top, front corner, first cutting round the adjacent sides of the cylinder and sphere.

The cylinder can now be rounded; and again, because of the slope of the table, it will be very thin at the bottom and thick at the top. Also, because of the sloping side of the cube, the left-hand side of the cylinder will be deeper than the right. A similar effect is experienced in the case of the sphere.

The top of the cylinder is sloped backwards in the same way as the top of the cube. A better effect will be achieved if the edges are slightly undercut, especially round the sphere and cylinder. (See cross section at Fig. 51).

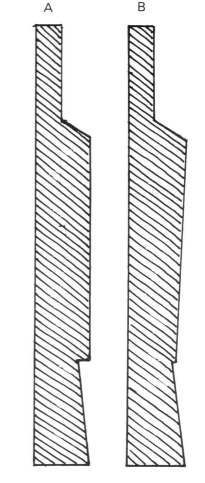

A   B

Fig. 50

Fig. 51

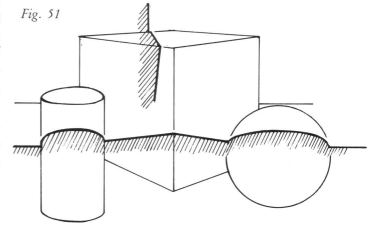

After careful sanding, the impression is not bad. (Fig. 52). It can be seen that the sphere is the least successful, appearing to have little volume. This is, I think, because the sphere has no perspective and no cue to its depth. Although it is commonly believed that perspective gives the impression of distance and recession, research has shown that in fact depth cues do most of this work. For example, the top of the cylinder is an elipse, which is usually a circle seen from an angle. Although the cylinder could actually be oval in section, it is most unlikely and our brain interprets the seen shape as a cylinder seen from an angle, thereby giving depth to the carving. In the same way, the long diamond shape on the top of the cube is interpreted, not as some oddly shaped rhomboidal solid, but as an oblique view of a cube. These factors do not work in favour of the sphere which looks identical from any angle. Had it been replaced by, say, a pyramid, suitably positioned, the overall effect could have been enhanced. This shows once again, the need to plan a relief with great care and forethought.

Fig. 52

LOW RELIEF, ADVANCED WORK – DOG'S HEAD

Having completed the exercise in modelling techniques you now have to make a choice of a subject to carve. Look for something bold and simple without a great deal of small detail and intricate shapes which will make reducing the background difficult. For example, plants are often attempted, but the problems of cutting out the shapes between the stems and leaves and setting-in the background areas are very severe. An animal or a simple still life is far easier and can be carved on a scale approximating reality which enables you to make a direct comparison of shapes.

I decided to carve a dog's head from a photograph, (Fig. 53), which was large enough to trace directly onto the wood.

Notice that the shape is fairly simple and one with which we are all familiar. The profile view is the most characteristic and easily recognisable, and although the open mouth might look problematic, it is, in fact, quite straight forward and helps to suggest depth by deep hollowing. Fig. 54.

The background is removed to a depth of 12mm ($\frac{1}{2}''$) and the outline set–in vertically. Fig. 55. Next the neck, top of the head, nose and lower jaw are rounded. Where the neck meets the body it is simply faded away. This is to overcome the problem mentioned before of the panel ending up thicker at the bottom than the top. The tongue is cut across at an angle and the upper lip undercut. The ear is undercut on the outside edges and slopes inwards to the hole or the inside. The boney lump of the eye is roughly shaped and the folds running under the throat indicated. (Fig. 56.) To say "that's all there

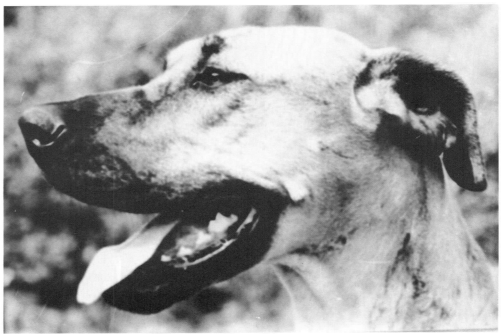

Fig. 53

Fig. 54

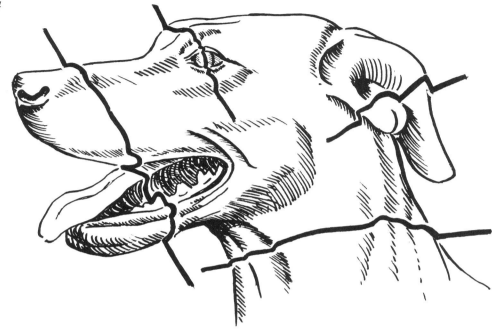

Fig. 55

Fig. 56

is to it" would be a great simplification, but, as can be seen from the photograph of the finished panel, Fig. 57, the shape is there, needing only a few details to complete it.

This is a classical medallion profile pose, and, having tried it, it is easy to see why the side view is always used. Apart from a slight foreshortening of the eye and some difficult undercutting to get behind the teeth, it is almost like carving half a head as in figure carving. (You may also like to refer back to Chapter One to the illustrations of 'Colonel Blood' and 'Brendan'.)

Fig. 57

CHAPTER FOUR

High Relief

Progressing from low relief to high relief is a major step and requires considerably rethinking the whole process. For a start, the background becomes too deep for the average router, so far more labour is involved in removing waste. Also the levels and angles become more complex, so the use of the router is even less likely. Because the subjects are more realistic in shape and depth the representation of natural perspective requires less intuitive decision making but the technical problems of undercutting and shaping become far more difficult.

STILL LIFE – GLASS, CHEESE-BOARD AND BOTTLE

Set up a still life and draw it onto a 45mm (1¾″) thick limewood board. The background area of greatest depth is cut away first, leaving 6mm (¼″) of wood. Next, the tabletop is carved, as in the previous still life, sloping from front to back. (Fig. 58). However, because the cheese-board is higher than the table top, the table must be dropped by 6mm (¼″) or so at the front edge. All the other objects must be cut in square and left standing proud of the table. These can now be separated by cutting-in around the glass,

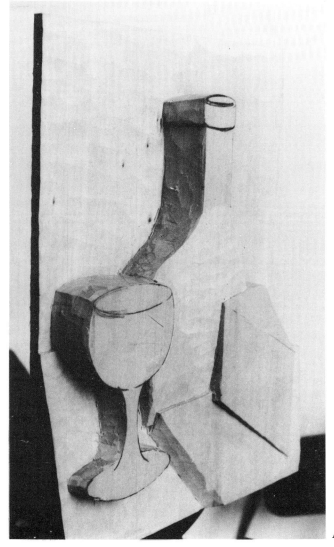

Fig. 58

cheese and board, and having done that the bottle can be rounded, going behind the other pieces. The top of the bottle neck is, of course, elliptical and can be hollowed out slightly. The glass is now rounded and shaped, and, as with the cylinder in the previous exercise, it must get smaller towards the base as it returns into the sloping table top. (Fig. 59).

Similarly, the side of the cheese must slope downwards to meet the cheese-board, whilst the top of it slopes backwards. The left edge of the cheese-board then becomes a problem. To keep the corner of it away from the bottle, it must be angled outwards. If it is cut in on a near natural angle, like the side of the cheese, it would appear thicker. The compromise is to change the angle slightly as it moves down the carving, giving it a

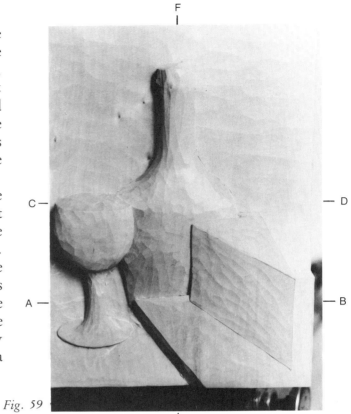

Fig. 59

Fig. 60

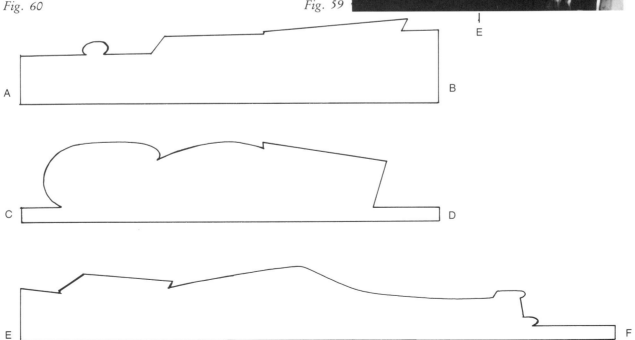

slight twist. This sounds confusing but the cross sections (Fig. 60) should clarify it. All the back edges can be heavily undercut. On these simple shapes this is relatively easy, but when carving flowers or figures it can be extremely difficult. It has been said that undercutting is the test of the carver's ability; it is, certainly, a great trial of patience, clean cutting and the skillful use of tools.

As an exercise this works very well and the carver should gain valuable experience from the problems involved in such a piece. My overall impression of my carving, shown finished in Fig. 61, is that it has a strange, disconcerting appearance but this is something which can be noted, analysed and may suggest further experiment and exploitation in other carvings.

Always try to observe which techniques and effects work well and which are unsuccessful, and benefit from them in future work.

Fig. 61

HIGH RELIEF, ADVANCED WORK – OWL IN FLIGHT

High relief is the most complex and sophisticated form of relief and the one which offers the most interesting possibilities. As in the case of the dog's head in low relief, it is wise to start with a fairly simple subject and one which is easily recognisable for what it is. It is very easy to see a picture of a bird or animal which, because of the perfection of photography, looks ideal for a carving, but is not, in fact, displaying the typical features of the subject. The owl, for example, is easily recognised full face, whilst most birds are more easily identified by the side views.

Although the owl is more complex than the dog, being smaller and more detailed, it is still basically one single shape on a flat background with the smaller features within that shape. What is radically different between the dog and owl is that in the latter we are attempting to include as much as possible of the bird's body in three dimensions, whilst in the former, there is no suggestion of carving anything which is not visible on the two dimensional photograph.

The possibility of portraying birds in flight is one of the most exciting possibilities of relief carving. The bird could, after all, be joined to the background or sky by a very small "pillar" of wood at the back, virtually invisible from a normal viewing position, thus raising the bird away from the panel and effectively making it fly, although in this example, I have not gone to these lengths.

The picture used is taken from Eric Hosking's *Owls* and I was tempted to put in some of the features in the composition, such as a church spire or branches, but finally decided that the plain expanse of empty wood gave the bird a certain feeling of flight. By the same token, I feel one must be a little free with the timber to provide that large expanse, and that entails a lot of work to remove the waste and since this is a good 45mm (1½") deep, the router is not very effective.

There are other ways of removing the waste area quickly – even a chainsaw might find its place in your workshop on occasions. Normally a large gouge and heavy mallet

Fig. 62

are best, but when the areas are small and restricted large drills might be used; (see Minotaur). I decided to run the panel across a circular saw repeatedly (although an overhead radial saw would have been even better), until the waste could be chipped away in large blocks. The area immediately around the bird had, of course, to be done in the normal way. Then the whole background was tooled to a smooth surface. Fig. 62.

The owl itself, like most reliefs, is a mixture of high and low areas. The rather flat face of the bird (Fig. 63) is almost natural, as are the legs and feet. The wings are, perhaps, half their natural depth whilst the body is very compressed. Fig. 64a and 64b.

Fig. 63

Fig. 64c

Fig. 64

The drawing shows the wing heavily undercut on the upper side and deeply scooped out underneath. The feathers are treated simply as overlapping scales on the wings and tail. The cross section, Fig. 64c, shows the legs almost three dimensional and becoming more undercut towards the feet. The lower edges of the wings and tail are very shallow, but sharply undercut. Figs 65 and 66.

The overall impression of this is quite good (Fig. 67), and the idea of the owl hanging in the empty sky, has, I think, been conveyed.

The side view, of course, shows the body to be somewhat compressed but this can be altered by using thicker timber, or, perhaps, by putting the carving into a deep frame. The final positioning and viewing angles of a relief must always be considered and, if necessary, adjustments made – such as framing – to get the best from the finished work. This exercise should also convey to the carver, the possibilities for portraying not only flight, but many subjects too fragile, unsupported or disjointed to be attempted in the round.

Fig. 65

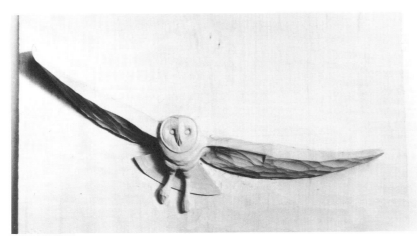

Fig. 66

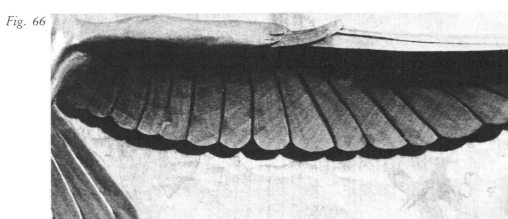

Fig. 67 By courtesy of Mr and Mrs R. Mann

HIGH RELIEF, ADVANCED WORK – NUDE

As stated earlier, in relief more attention must be paid to design in order to maximise the potential of the depth of the wood available to create a three dimensional illusion. To carve this nude I first looked for a piece of timber with a pronounced straight grain, my idea being that the three dimensional qualities of this figure would be accentuated by the straight grain of the flat background contrasting with the curved and contoured grain on the relief. I used ash, but pitch pine or certain other softwoods, such as cypress, might also be used.

In trying to design this relief to work effectively I found that it imposed strict limitations on the work. Apart from using ash, which is a miserable wood to carve, I also arranged that the finished carving was to be lit by an angle-poise lamp shining from the top left-hand side. This meant that most of the decision work must be done at night. Also, because the carving was to be lit from the same direction, the light-facing surface should be sloped more to catch the light whilst the shaded side be more curved to form shadow. Fig. 68.

In practise I found, once again, that there are no formulas for relief carving. For instance, the shadow on the right side of the torso must be angled to accentuate the ribs and the muscle of the stomach and slope quite gradually to the right to show the side of the body. The left, lit side, must slope much more sharply because there is simply no room for a long slope. This moves the highlights, so the angle must be slightly altered again.

I designed the ponytail to hang behind the head to provide another depth cue. The ribbon was introduced to wrap around the hands and lay over the legs so that the depth of these features could be shown by the shape of the strip round them. This is a well known principle and acts in the same way and for the same reason the people will avoid wearing horizontally striped clothes.

The little platform is introduced to give some straight lines to offset the many curved ones and to give lines of perspective on its top. These are slightly exaggerated, tapering more than they should. Fig. 69.

The overall plan then, is a system of levels: the hanging cloth tapering back to the right leg, this overlapping the left leg; the left hand disappearing behind the knee; the right arm overlaying the upper back; the chest sloping away, one breast full face, the other in profile, seen in front of the left arm. Again, the face in profile looking slightly behind the legs into space; the hair overlays the forehead and the skull in front of the ponytail. Against this the ribbon gives "visible proof" of the three dimensional shapes and the oval background, smaller than the figure, allowing it to exist in space with a tangible object – perhaps a mirror or window – somewhere in the distance behind it. I think it is seldom that one works so

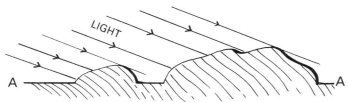

Fig. 68 Section A through left arm and body showing how the direction of light falls on the carving.

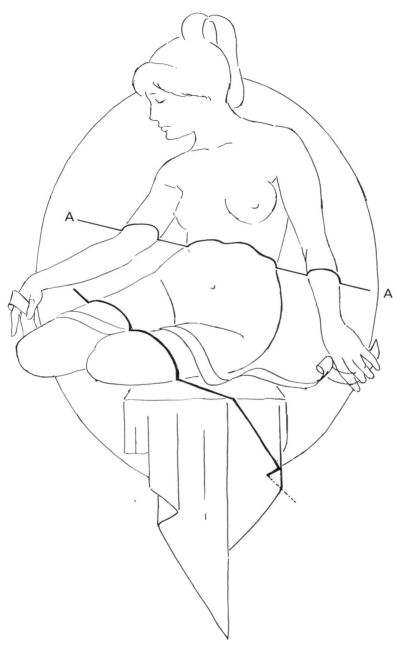

Fig. 69

Fig. 70 The drawn-up block is bandsawn to shape and routed.

like a side view of the right breast. This is not so obvious as it sounds. The foreshortening of the right breast will not be totally convincing; it will appear slightly flat. Therefore, the left breast must be made slightly flatter than it should be, to match the right. Fig. 72. The carving of the head is straight forward enough, as are the arms. The fingers of the left hand are carefully hidden behind the forefinger and thumb which are virtually natural. Those of the right hand have to be foreshortened from the second knuckle to the tips. The right leg, which in fact points quite sharply forward, is considerably fore-

Fig. 71

hard to contrive a piece but the academicians of the past did so as the norm. Perhaps that is why we find many of their works uninspiring.

On the practical side, I bandsawed the block and routed out as much as I could of the background and cut the rest by hand, Fig. 70. I then roughed out the main areas of the body, lowering the left arm and leg, rounding the torso and head. Fig. 71. I went to great pains to make the left breast look

Fig. 72

shortened and this is quite crucial. Study the work of old masters to get some idea. Most women's thighs are pretty smooth, bland pieces of flesh. More muscular structure must be introduced to enable you to indicate distances along its length. Also, the structure of the knee must be rendered accurately or it will look grotesque. Over all this the ribbon must wind its way, exaggerating slightly the thinness and thickness to enhance the perspective. The section where it bridges the table and hand is, of course, difficult technically and requires great care. Fig. 73. The cloth is quite straightforward but needs undercutting.

Ash is difficult to sand because the soft lines of grain tend to tear out with the coarser grades of sandpaper. However, it is quite pleasing when finished. I left the wood with a fairly dull finish. (Fig. 74).

Fig. 73

Fig. 74

PIERCED HIGH RELIEF – THE GREEN MAN

A pierced relief is one in which parts of the carving are cut right through the wood, creating a kind of shaped hole, usually revealing a dark cavity; or it can simply be a carved, pierced frame for a picture, or as part of a chairback, for example. It is not really the same as a fretted carving such as a Chippendale ribbon-back chair or the screens found in Moorish buildings, where so much wood has been cut away as to leave only a thin lattice work.

Piercing gives a definite richness and depth to a relief, as can be seen on the Jacobean mouldings frequently found in churches. Here a false front is made to cover a hollow space, which is then carved and pierced, the holes opening onto the dark cavity behind.

I have used the idea of piercing on a kind of boss which might be applied to a door or simply hung on the wall. The subject is the Green Man, or Jack O'Green, an ancient fertility symbol featuring a man with leaves growing out of his body. This enabled me to carve a character portrait whichever way I chose and did not dictate any particular design to the leaves such as a traditional pattern might. (Some of the stylised traditional foliage designs can be very exacting and not a little boring.) Fig. 75.

Fig. 75

Fig. 76

Fig. 77

Fig. 78

Fig. 79

In a design such as this the first stage is to cut out a disc about 200mm (8″) diameter and 100mm (4″) thick. (I used oak because it seemed suitable for an old world subject.) This disc is hollowed out at the back leaving about 25mm (1″) of thickness (Fig. 76). Next the front of the block is rounded off to make a hollow dome, Fig. 77. The corners of the pentagram are then cut in since they are fixed points, whilst the foliage can be changed and shaped around them. Now the outline of the face can be shaped, obviously leaving the nose as the highest point, and a deep vee cut at the point where the face meets the leaves. Don't forget to allow for the branches coming from the mouth. Fig. 78.

Fig. 80

Fig. 81

Now you can start to rough in the shapes of the leaves and stems, using a drill to pierce the holes through to the hollow inside. Quite quickly they should begin to look like Fig. 79 at the front and Fig. 80 at the back. The chopping out of these holes and hollows is not as difficult as it may appear. Some use of spoonbent gouges is necessary and if you have flexible shaft and burrs (6mm ($\frac{1}{4}$″) ball ended) the work will be greatly facilitated.

What is difficult, is to achieve a reasonable tooled finish and to cut clean corners where the undercuts stop. Figs. 81 shows the refining of the face and for further ideas I would recommend the study of old master paintings and, perhaps, gargoyles on churches. The finish I used was a dark oak stain followed by a coat of brown shellac sealer and brown wax polish. (Fig. 82).

Fig. 82 By courtesy of Mr D.C.C. Wilson.

Fig. 83

APPLIED HIGH RELIEF – ROSE

Graham Thomson of The Lilacs Nursery, Evesham, is one of England's remaining handful of commercial rose growers. This beautiful rose, Fig. 83, grown by him seemed to me an excellent subject with which to show the technique of applying a relief to the background, instead of cutting it out of the block.

Fretting a relief and gluing it to the ground is a tried and tested traditional technique, and one which offers interesting possibilities of using contrasting woods; building up a carving in layers, as in much of the work of Grinling Gibbons, and of applying carvings to other objects – furniture, boxes, etc. Of course, it can also be used simply to facilitate carving a complex or delicate high relief, as in the case of this rose which is glued to a background of the same wood.

Applied reliefs can appear "stuck on" but this can be overcome by avoiding brash combinations of ill-contrasting or badly matched timbers. Indeed, for a perfect result the carving could be cut from one half of a board, split through its thickness, the surfaces having been planed ready for gluing, the one piece could then be fretted, carved and glued back in its original position, thereby ensuring that the grain matched perfectly. Only the keenest eye would recognise the difference.

The first stage in carving the rose is to make it in modelling clay. The reason for this is that it is the easiest way to find out what the back looks like where it is pressed against the background. Also, the real rose would be too floppy to use as a model over several days. Fig. 84.

Make the model and press it on to a flat board, then carefully remove it and turn it over. Now the fretted piece of walnut is glued face down onto a board with paper inserted between the two surfaces of the glue so that the carving can be easily split away. The back of the rose is now carved using the back of the clay model to copy from. Fig. 85. Be sure to make this work as complete as possible, shaping the stem and leaves as much as you can. Once the rose is removed from the board it will be virtually impossible to do any further carving on the back. Using a thin knife, carefully prise the rose away from the board and re-glue it temporarily, face up, so that work can continue on the front. Carving the flower and leaves down to the final thickness will require very sharp tools and a gentle touch.

Fig. 84

Fig. 85

Carefully sand this part when completed, remove the carving from the board and sand those areas of the back that will show. Finish with two coats of shellac, a light rub down and wax polish.

The background in my example was a piece of walnut veneered blockboard from a 1930's wardrobe door; this was polished and the rose glued to it. (Be sure to scrape away all wax from the points of contact when gluing pieces together.) A walnut frame was fitted, completing a very presentable piece. Figs. 86 and 87.

Fig. 87

Fig. 86 By courtesy of Mr and Mrs P. Parkin.

CHAPTER FIVE

Relief Carving as a Sculptural Art

In the foregoing chapters I have several times referred to the "possibilities" and "potential uses" of relief carving and I hope that the next few projects will give some idea of what I mean by that. Whilst I am a follower of tradition in my work I do believe that the concept behind the tradition must advance with the society it is displayed to, even though the subject may be an old one. For example, one might well carve a gladiator from 2,000 years ago, but the approach to it, our ideas about war and combat, even our understanding of human anatomy and psychology will produce a different carving than would a Victorian, Roman, Renaissance or Art Nouveau sculptor.

In the second half of the 20th century we have seen great developments in the visual arts ranging from computer graphics to holograms to kinetic sculptures, and so on. Many types of media may be employed in one piece of work, and styles range from naturalism through surrealism to total abstraction, and any combination in between.

Within the limitations of relief sculpture there is no reason why the same freedom cannot be exercised. Today, no-one will raise their eyebrows at the use of paints and stains, burning, sandblasting, using strange combinations of wood with other materials or whatever. Also, diverging from naturalism, distortion of perspective and scale, roughly hewn or highly finished – all have their uses.

I hope that many beginners will see that using their imagination well can be a great compensation for the lack of skill they may initially have.

MARILLION

Although this piece was commissioned and I had personally never heard the music of Marillion, I immediately felt that their record cover was an exciting subject for a relief carving. It is not technically difficult, but there are some interesting problems. For example, the right-hand side of the face showing through the translucent mask; the strange clouds going both behind and in front of the body, and the fading of the shoulder into the sky. These kind of effects may necessitate the use of unconventional methods of carving or the use of more than one kind of relief – for example, incised in combination with high or low relief; texturing surfaces with punches or scrapers may suggest different qualities and materials. For me, half the pleasure of carving is finding ways to cope with these kind of difficulties. Figs. 88 and 89 show the record sleeve and my drawing.

Fig. 88

Fig. 89

I chose a piece of 25mm (1″) walnut from the crotch of a tree where the grain was wild and swirling and the white sapwood showed in an irregular patch; factors which I hoped would contribute to the contrasting lights and shadows. I also decided to carve it within its own frame to create a kind of window effect. This does however create considerably more work.

The first stage is to waste the sky, that is the area along the line of clouds on the right, around the head and back of the collar to the clouds on the left. This is taken down 19mm (¾″) with the router. The lettering is simply left as a block. Now look for the highest areas of the carving. The tassel and

bell, and the cheek of the mask would probably stand highest (see Fig. 90 Section A-A), therefore cut round the edges of the mask and roughly shape it. The area covering the face is lowered about 6mm (¼″), going deeper and deeper towards the neck and shoulder. The clouds covering the shoulder are left high. Next, shape the hanging tassel, the cap and the pointed flaps. These are sharply undercut to separate them from the sky. The modelling of the face can now proceed. Start by deeply undercutting the edge of the mask and reduce the face to go under it. The deep furrows of the cheek are cut in, and the throat disappearing under the clouds can be cut to the lowest level of

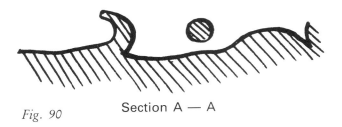

Fig. 90   Section A — A

The clouds are rather difficult and tedious. I tried using a burr to achieve the ragged edge but found the semi-circular scoops too mechanical. Those more pronounced on the left were carefully outlined with small gouges. Notice that the upper level on the extreme left overlap the shoulder, whilst the dark patch (hatched in the drawing, Fig 89,)

the whole carving (Fig. 90, Section A-A). The hollow of the mouth is cut very deeply to produce a dark shadow, as is the nostril. The use of rotary burrs could be a distinct advantage here, and at the edge of the mask. Very fine work must be carried out on the eyelashes, perhaps using a knife or scalpel. The actual iris is incised at the edge and rounded, Fig. 91, and a sharp off-centre hole made for the pupil, then a tiny semi-circle is cut for the highlight.

Fig. 92

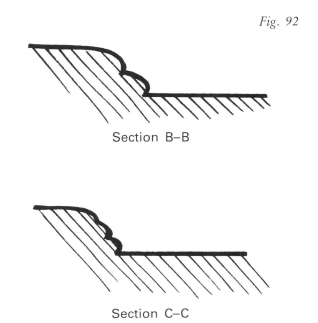

Section B–B

Section C–C

Fig. 91

The work is fairly straightforward, the only real difficulty being the far cheek and eye which must be "overlapped" by the nose and lips. (Fig. 92 Sections B-B and C-C). The mask eyehole is cut in deeply and undercut with a rotary burr. The right-hand side of the jester's face shows through the translucent mask. I decided to suggest this by outlining the profile with the very slightest indentation in the wood. Fig. 93.

are cut into it. Also, some of the clouds go behind the stick on the mask and others go in front of it. The very complex cloud on the right, is done with a vee tool, rocking it from side to side to achieve the ragged lines. You can also carve a kind of corrugated surface into the sky along the lines of the "rays" emanating from the distant clouds. Careful sanding follows, particularly of the mask, whilst the sky is left with a slightly sanded, tooled finish.

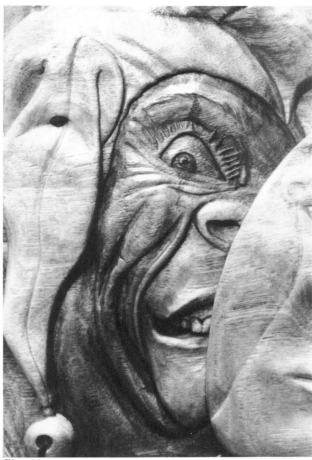

Fig. 93

smooth, the wood grain completely filled. When the polish is thoroughly hardened, rub it over with a paste metal polish, which makes it shine like plate glass. The interior of the mask's eyehole is carefully painted with dark brown shellac to increase the "depth" of the hole. The rest of the carving is brushed over with a mid-brown shellac sealer, except for the jester's eye, on which a clear polish can be used to keep it light. The clouds are sanded again to remove the brown shellac from their high points. The idea of this is to heighten the tonal differences between the dark shadows and light clouds. Other parts of the relief are carefully shaded with dark brown shellac sealer using a soft sable brush – particularly the darker parts of the face, the iris, and the shoulder, and the upper parts of the sky. The triangular make-up area on the upper and lower lids are marked in by punching and the punched area then slightly darkened. Finally the whole carving is waxed, and the outside frame given five or six coats of matt black paint, carefully rubbed down and polished.

The purist might say that coloured paint on a face has no physical depth or thickness and therefore should not be on the carving. One would not normally, for example, "carve" the pattern on a piece of clothing. However, it could also be argued that there is no actual hole in the pupil of an eye, so that should not be carved, but when the eyes have no pupils they appear blind. I think the answer is that if you feel that the detail is important, put it in anyway you feel is acceptable. Similarly, you may feel a carving would look more effective with an "antique" finish, which can be quite easily achieved by applying dark wax with a brush

I considered polishing to be an integral part of the carving, which I hoped would enhance not only the wood, which is usually the case, but also the pictorial effect. The mask and the bell, I wanted to be highly polished, as on the original picture. The method of achieving this, if you are not adept at french polishing, is as follows: give the wood a brush coat of clear cellulose sealer and when dry rub down with 400 grit paper. Then give it five or six more coats, between each rubbing down most delicately. After six coats the surface should be silky and then wiping most of it off with a cloth, leaving the dark only in the corners. There are many instances when a touch of colour in a hole such as a mouth or nose, will improve the effect of hollowness. These methods need experimentation and trial before use, but can greatly improve a carving.

Much of the success of this piece must lie with the beauty of the figured walnut. In limewood, for example, the whole impression would be different, though not necessarily bad. However, I do think this piece particularly shows the value of selecting a suitable piece of timber.

The carved name is dealt with in the later chapter on lettering.

Fig. 94 By courtesy of the owner D. Winlow Esq., and by kind permission of the original record sleeve designer Mark Wilkinson, and with thanks to the group Marillion for the use of their name.

THE BOX OF DELIGHTS

I have attempted to develop the concept of an all round relief carving in the form of a series of separate panels, integrated by the relationships between the subject content of the individual pieces and by their physical proximity on adjacent sides. They maintain independence from each other by physical separation on the square block, which of course prohibits the viewer from seeing more than a part of the whole at any one time, and by being in the form of friezes, layered vertically with bands of lettering between them. Such is the effect of the written word that it is difficult for the audience to engage all their attention on the illustrations without focussing on, and interpreting, the text. If these bands were merely ornament, I believe this would not be so.

The theme of the carvings is not intended to be of religious significance although it may have some biblical content. It is intended more as a satirical, perhaps slightly cynical view of the life cycle as it was propounded in bygone days by the moralizers of the Christian Church, in order to keep the peasantry under the thumb. I flatter myself that I may have a little of the humour of the misericord carvers of the medieval period, if not their skill.

The sphere at the top, turned from thuya root burr represents the world held in a claw (Fig. 95). Below it are two serpents entwined in a Celtic knot, one having a forked tongue, the other having a single tongue, vaguely representing good and evil. Evil, of course, will out, and below the serpents are the deadly sins in the form of faces (over page) carved in yew, laburnum, box, olive, cherry, plum, walnut and folha de bola. These are quite fascinating to do, and one could spend many satisfying hours finding faces and expressions to match various moods and sentiments. Their names are inscribed above them in an alphabet designed by Albrecht Durer.

Fig. 95

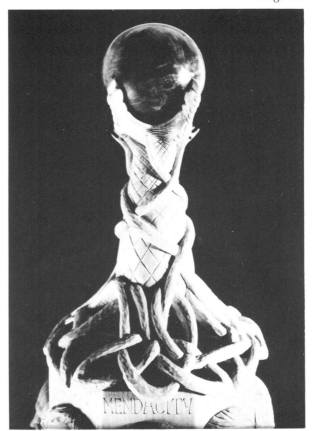

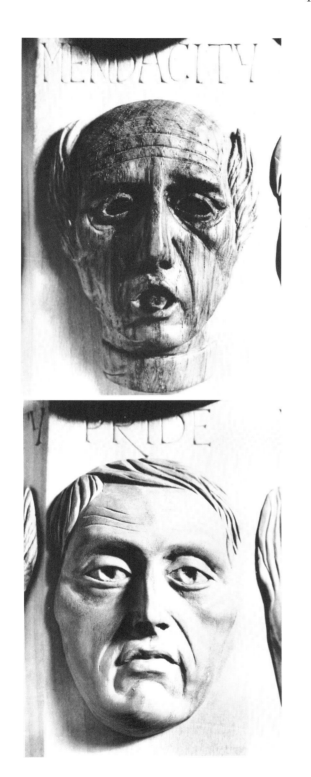

Fig. 96

On the next panel (Fig. 97), a rather jolly looking Devil rushes through a wood in pursuit of a young female who has disappeared around the corner. The Jester peers from behind a tree, laughing at the Devil's efforts to corrupt the totally corrupt, and waves his bladder at him. A line from the Book of Revelations is carved under the panel "Let him that has understanding count the number of the beast".

Fig. 97

The next feature is an inscription in Fraktur designed in 1794, by Johann Gubitz which reads "What reward shall be given to thee false tongue". Below this are four panels, the first depicting Eve (Fig. 96), sat under the tree holding an apple, and looking a little pleased with herself. In the branches, the serpent, with the head of a jester, laughs at the storm that is about to break and at Eve's defence in the inscription below: "The serpent did beguile me and I did eat".

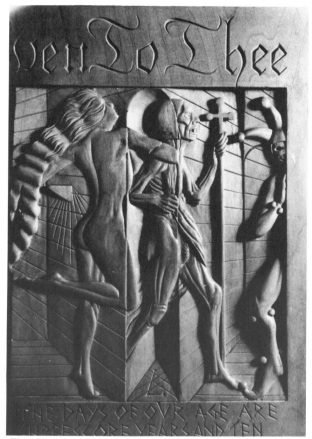

Fig. 98

Finally, on the fourth side (Fig. 99) King Death waits with open arms; an hour-glass in one hand and a sword in the other. Behind him, receding perspectives of emptiness vanish into a doorway. Like a rising sun, the Jester's head appears behind the door, mocking even death. Below this panel is written "There was a door to which I found no key", from the Rubaiyat of Omar Khayyam. No key is needed to enter the House of Death.

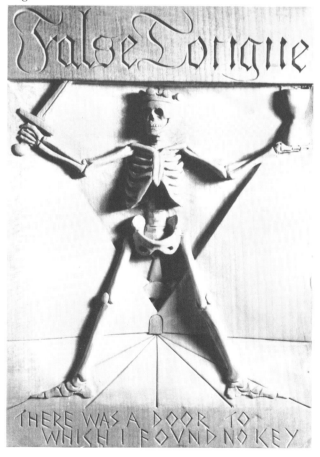

Fig. 99

The pursued lady is featured on the next side (Fig. 98) running friskily into a doorway, from which she appears as a shrivelled old woman, who, being no longer desired for sin, has taken the cross. On the left, a sundial counts away the fleeting moments of youth, and on the right the Jester smirks at the new found religion of the old hag: "The days of our age are three score years and ten" is inscribed below.

Fig. 100

Fig. 101

The final frieze around the base depicts purgatory – no fire and brimstone but a Never-Never Land where the personality is destroyed, symbolised by a distorted head (Fig. 100); individuality and choice are removed, symbolised by two bodies floating in space (Fig. 101), and the joy and richness of life ceases to exist – of the Jester,

Fig. 102

Fig. 103

only the grinning skull remains (Fig. 102). However, on the fourth side, (Fig. 103) a girl with a secretive, mischievious smile, holds out hope for those who have played their cards right. Even in hell there will be priviledged classes.

The purpose of all this, is, in fact, to decorate and conceal a secret draw inside the block which can only be opened by removing various hidden catches, which are to be found by following the clues in the text.

The carvings are, basically, fairly simple and shallow reliefs. They are all experiments of some kind: foreshortening in the case of the floating bodies; perspective in the backgrounds of the King Death and Old Age panels, the movement of the Devil contrasted against the straight trees and ground.

The lettering is also a development from other carvings I have done which included lettering. It can be very simple, such as the inscriptions above the bottom frieze, which is adapted from ancient Greek and Phoenician styles, and requires only one or two small, flat chisels; or highly complex like the almost unreadable bottom line, which is 15th century English, nearly all done with a vee tool. In fact, it says "Fools, your reward is neither here nor there". (Omar Khayyam).

What must be stressed is that relief carvings must be designed to work. As I have said previously, the front view of a face is more difficult than the side view – there is a limit to how much it can be squashed before it ceases to function as an image of a normal face. On the other hand, the figure shown floating head-forward shows the gross foreshortening that can be effectively conveyed in 12 millimetres of wood.

As a project the box is an ambitious one, taking many days work, but it is built of small parts, none of which is particularly difficult – it relies on the total conception to have its effect. This is a good principle to work by. Many carvings appear to be daunting in their size or complexity but most are only the sum of the parts. Fig. 104 shows the finished carving

Fig. 104 By courtesy of
Mr D.C.C. Wilson

MIDSUMMER NIGHT'S DREAM

I have never inclined to the view taken by some wood sculptors that the individual pieces of timber should dictate or even suggest the subject and treatment of a carving. My attitude has always been that the piece is designed on paper and then applied to a suitable block of wood. This of course means that, timber supplies being limited, the material available even for small carvings may not be entirely suitable. My attitude was changed somewhat by Charles Boren of Fort Worth, Texas, who chops a piece off a dead tree when he sees possibilities in its natural conformation and alters his treatment of it to suit the grain and characteristics he finds while working it.

It certainly made me think more about the character of the wood and its relationship to the subject, and although I still design a carving on paper, I do it bearing in mind a

Fig. 105

particular piece of timber I have available.

The piece of walnut used for this carving was cut from a large butt because of a section of decay. It was chainsawn out, like a huge wedge of cheese and virtually thrown away, to be bought by myself at firewood price.

I set myself the task of using this rough block as a basis of a relief carving which would get away from the notion of the picture type panel and into the idea of a three dimensional, walk-around relief carving –

a kind of halfway house between in-the-round carving and relief. (Figs 105 and 106)

This of course, is not a new idea – the Elgin marbles, for instance, depict a continuing scene around an entire building. Many pieces of applied art are decorated with reliefs which are seen from all round. However, I think considerable use could be made of this type of all-round relief as a sculpture in itself, where one part would relate to another unseen part, or perhaps

Fig. 106

Fig. 107

combine with a three dimensional sculpture. I have extended this idea to some extent in the previous project "Box of Delights"

Originally the theme was "A Midsummer Night's Dream" featuring characters and events from Shakespeare's play. I started with the theatrical mask one end and a rather unpleasant looking "putto" appearing from behind it, representing Puck. A Greek helmet symbolises Theseus, Duke of Athens, and a group of long, thin trees, the forest. Around this point I began to deviate from the story of the play and move towards the atavism and eroticism that seemed to underly

Fig. 108

it. This led to the head of Pan peering from the branches, and with the little demons at the top, and frogs below. (Figs. 107 and 108). Without trying to analyse everything on the carving or pretend that it has some deep meaning, I would simply call this a carved doodle allowing one's mind to wander and putting it down in wood. It is a very pleasant and easy way to carve, without having to conform to designs, scale or accuracy. (Further detail is illustrated overpage)

Walnut is an ideal wood for such a thing, capable of fine detail and yet displaying beautiful grain and colour on broader areas.

The variety of subject matter and the depth of undercutting in some sections necessitated a large range of tools. Virtually every kind of carving tool was employed as well as knives, rotary burrs, drill, files, rasps, abrasives and even a chain saw to cut the deep incisions between the trees.

I would certainly never suggest that anyone try to copy this carving, but as a starting point I think it is a fascinating project to undertake for anyone with a little "self expression" trying to get out.

Figs. 109 and 110 Detail from Fig. 106

Fig. 111. Detail from Fig. 106

MINOTAUR

The subject of perspective and the illusion of depth is one which has fascinated many people since the Renaissance. It is very interesting to reflect on the fact that the whole concept of perspective in art is only about 500 years old, and that for the previous three or four thousand years it was totally ignored. It is hard to believe that the highly sophisticated sculptors of the ancient world were incapable of reproducing the appearance of distance. However, bearing in mind the fact that perspective is not a necessity, there is no doubt that it becomes almost obsessive when you get involved in it.

The theme of the Minotaur, incarcerated inside a maze of tunnels has interested a number of sculptors and painters. I felt it would be interesting to try to create a suggestion of this subterranean world in a relatively small area; in other words, there would be a 75–100mm (3–4″) thick board of wood, carved in such a way that the scene would appear far deeper than the wood thickness itself. The scene would be viewed through an opening. Obviously, to carve a hollow cave through a small opening would be very difficult. To get round this I intended

to make the block in two parts so that the tunnels could be carved into each piece which would then be screwed together. (Fig. 112).

Another problem would be the darkness inside the cave. At first I intended to insert small electric bulbs into the wood but later decided to use perspex rods.

I made a plaster model first (Fig. 113) to work out some of the design problems. It is not so easy to position arches, columns and passages so that they overlap enough to give the feeling of depth whilst not obscuring the areas behind them. Certain effects seem to work better than others – spiral staircases and long corridors being quite effective.

I chose a large slab of 100mm (4″) walnut for the carving, with a small piece for the back half. I carved out the front arches which formed the entrance to the labyrinth and then, using a 25mm (1″) saw tooth drill, began to deepen them. This facade is based on the neolithic buildings at Gozo near Malta.

These recesses were then drilled deeper, carved and shaped until the slab was pierced through. (Fig. 114). Work was then continued from the back of the block (Fig. 115);carving the back half of the piece is

Fig. 112

Fig. 113

Fig. 114

Fig. 115

Fig. 116

much easier since it is much shallower and open. The aperture of the back section is larger than that of the back opening of the front section. This eliminates the difficulty of marrying the two halves, and this is utilised to create an effect of separation between one area of the labyrinth and another (Fig. 116).

Fig. 117

Fig. 118

When the two parts of the carving were finished and screwed together certain areas were very dark; for example, the corridor on the left, the staircase in the centre and the rooms on the right (Fig. 117). Holes were drilled from above to these areas and perspex rods inserted. (These are shown in the photograph Fig. 116) The light source is a small neon striplight above the back half, behind the main block. These dark areas are then dimly lit from sources which appear to be out of sight, thereby implying some greater depth beyond that that is visible. Figs. 118 and 119.

Fig. 119

Fig. 120 By courtesy of Mr. K.P. Kelly

Finally, a small figure of the Minotaur was carved and inserted, not too obviously, into the tunnel. Fig. 120.

This carving does not photograph terribly well, but the general impression can be seen.

I do think that some experimentation with interior scenes, rather like the sort of thing Dutch painters were fond of, could prove fruitful, perhaps on a larger scale.

PRECINCT

Chip carving is a simple form of carving and very popular in Germany, Switzerland, Austria and the U.S.A. Also it can frequently be seen on antique oak furniture in Britain although it is no longer widely used. This, I believe, is mainly because wood carving is today seen more as an artistic activity in this country and chip carving is generally very repetitive, unimaginative, and seen, perhaps, as trivial.

Although I find it less than interesting it is a very good discipline for clean cutting. After all, virtually all carving is basically cutting chips of various shapes, and success depends on cutting them cleanly. It is carried out with chisels or special chip carving knives. Skew chisels are often used but an ordinary No. 1 will suffice much of the time.

The basic chip is an inverted pyramid cut in the manner shown in Figs. 122, 123, and 124. There are many variations on this basic

Fig. 12

Fig. 12

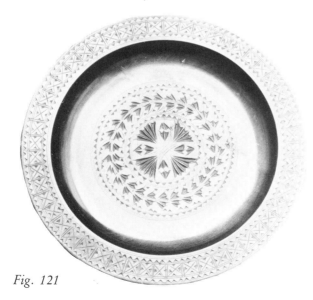

Fig. 121

Fig. 12

cut as seen in Fig. 121 and many excellent books explaining how it is done.

An additional, essential ingredient of a chip carving is lighting and this must be taken account of when planning your work. Because the carving cannot really be altered to suit the light, as a low relief could, there really needs to be a strong oblique source of light nearby to display the work to advantage. In diffused flourescent lighting it will be almost invisible. Only strong directional lighting from a low angle relative to the surface of the panel will bring out the true form of the relief. It may seem that I stress the subject of light sources, but it is common enough practice to light pictures individually and I am only recommending the same for carvings.

My interest is in using the *principle* of chip carving to achieve a pictorial effect which is secondary, or in addition to, the pattern of the actual cuts.

Using the geometrical paintings of Spyros Horeums (Figs. 125 and 126) as a basis for 'Precinct', I designed a relief where the pattern of chips carved on the flat surface would give an illusion of recession. However, to enhance the perception of perspective I have included a "depth cue" in the form of two figures; the near one pointing to the far one to lead the eye. This, of course, is a very obvious, almost naive contrivance, but one which illustrates the point quite clearly. Without the figures the pattern had depth and recession but no tangible relationship to the real world; by

Fig. 125

Fig. 126

including the figures it becomes a tunnel. The figures are simplified and in very low relief. They are symbols rather than realistic rendering of the human form. Of course, having people in the picture means having a floor for them to stand on, and also requires some material for their relief. This could be done either by gluing extra pieces of wood to the surface or by slightly lowering the background. I decided to make the entire panel in one great chip, i.e. an inverted pyramid, only about 12mm ($\frac{1}{2}''$) deep at the apex, but enough to give a shallow relief on the figures (Fig. 127).

To my dismay, I found that the wood I was using, Douglas fir, was extremely difficult and unpleasant to use, particularly when trying to get a clean cut straight from the chisel, an essential of chip carving. However, having achieved the raised figure, I set about the floor, carving it to look rather like uneven paving stones. You may find that using a sharp knife to cut the fibres and paring the chip away with a 12mm ($\frac{1}{2}$″) No. 2, works more easily than a flat chisel.

In this type of work, once the technique of cutting the chips is acquired, little difficulty should be experienced other than cleaning out the acute corners, using a skew or thin pointed knife. Obviously, smaller and smaller tools must be used towards the middle. The finish on this panel was a clear cellulose sealer followed by matt polyeurethane. Fig. 128 overpage shows the finished carving.

Fig. 127

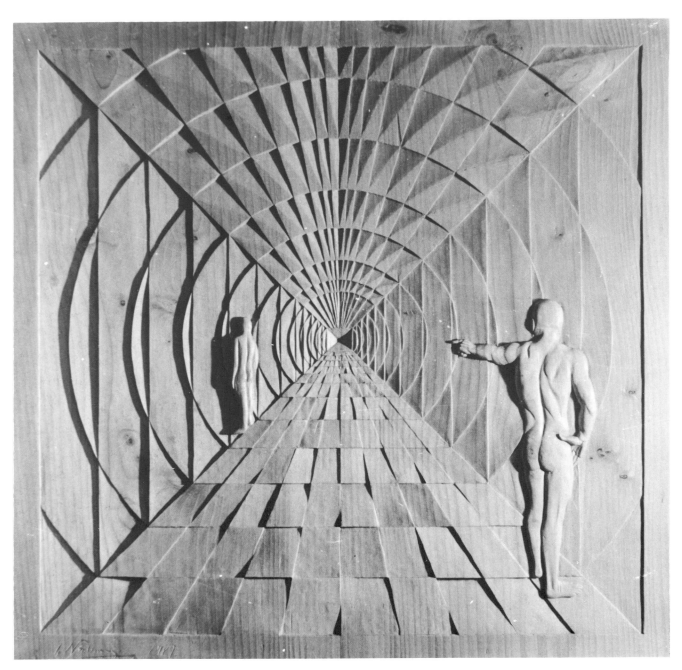

Fig. 128 (Courtesy of Mr and Mrs A.E. Penning).

CONCLUSIONS AND POSSIBILITIES

Tolstoy said of art "it is not a handicraft, it is a transmission of feeling, the artist has experienced". This I believe to be true, and conversely, if you remove the feeling you take away the art and are left with the handicraft. I have found relief carving at least a more adaptable form of communication and self-expression than three dimensional carving, if not a better one. In some ways, no doubt, the restrictions of carving in the round force you to think more about the content of what you make because only by the most carefully thought-out design will you be able to convey your idea. For example, it is very difficult indeed to carve an eagle swooping to the ground, wings spread, talons outstretched, about to seize its prey. These characteristics of the savage predator must be analysed and condensed into a more subtle form and incorporated into a study of the bird in a more stationary posture, probably sitting on a rock. However, with a relief carving, the subject can be exploited to the full, complete with mountain glen if required. One can easily see the pitfalls of becoming very pictorial, but one equally can see the potential.

Almost anything can be carved in relief, from the weirdest surrealism to the ultra traditional. As a means of communication it is almost the equal of painting. When you discover the exciting prospects of relief carving you may well wonder why there is so much attention paid to carving in the round.

Lettering, which is covered in the latter part of the book, is, admittedly, less open to dramatic effect, but the impact is more subtle. Ask any advertising agency. The precise style of letters, the way it is presented, the colour, the size and the position are all factors which make the audience react to a product in different ways. So too with carved lettering; even with a simple house sign, the treatment of the alphabet will alter our expectation of the house and its owners. I personally have a great fondness for incorporating lettering into sculptures. After all, chip carving, cut into specific shapes is lettering, they are both forms of relief carving, but the message is different. The name TUT-ANKH-AMUN on the Egyptian relief carries so much weight and underlying meaning – the whole history and mystery of ancient Egypt seems to be invoked by the word – that it gives the simple carving a completely different impact than if it were absent. Relief carving, and lettering, can be very simple; requiring no technical virtuosity, and be highly successful works of art, if the feeling is there. The way forward is through imagination and experiment.

CHAPTER SIX

Lettering

INCISED LETTERING

Roman capitals were, and still are, the greatest influence on the design and use of capital letters. The incised letters on the base of Trajan's column in Rome, cut in 114 AD, have stood as the classic standard of proportions and dignity for nearly 2,000 years and will probably continue to do so. Attempts to alter them have certainly not created improvements. These capitals were developed from the Greek alphabet, via the Etruscans. It is generally considered that the letters were painted onto the stone by an artist using a square tipped brush, held at a constant angle. This automatically produced the varying thickness of stroke and the serifs. The stonemason then incised the painted letter. These capitals were used for all writing, but being tedious to produce, the writers of manuscripts found an easier alphabet for general use called Rustica. The square capitals were henceforth only used for special pages, headings, and as initials. Today they serve as our capital letters. Fig. 129.

There is no exact system for constructing Trajan letters, though many great mathematicians and artists have tried to find one. The unique quality of the Roman capital does not mean it has to be slavishly copied.

Different times, different societies and changing requirements have produced inumerable alphabets and typefaces. The Roman, having been designed for carving in stone, lends itself admirably to carving in wood, and since it is still universally popular will be the basis for the first exercise here.

Just as there is no mechanical system for constructing Roman capitals there is no formula for spacing the letters or the words. Every word and every group of words presents a new problem and an aesthetic decision to be made. The beauty of the inscription, its readability, the whole impact of the thing, rests on these decisions, and this, allied to the actual cutting, is the art of letter carving. Only practice, experience, observations and perhaps luck can help you to succeed with the aesthetics; however the cutting can be learnt fairly easily.

The first stage towards letter carving is to obtain a printed alphabet and study it, copy it and get to know its geometry. I have found printed alphabets difficult to obtain but there are plenty of books on lettering in the shops and libraries. Roman, being the most commonly used is probably the best to begin with. The easiest subject for letter carving is a single word, such as a house name, on a board of unspecified length.

A 42° **V** 44° **W M** 52°

Full circle   Entasis — a slight convexity of lower half of strokes

O C G D Q

Inside oval on tilted axis

E F L B P R S

Ogee line   Serifs are a double ogee

K 90° **X** 54° **Y** 74°

H I J T U

N Z Slightly curved

Fig. 129

That means you can start drawing it out at one end and work along the board to the end of the word without having to work out whether or not it will fit in.

After years of carving lettering I now draw it straight onto the wood, but initially it is best to do an accurate, full size drawing on paper. You may find that you need to draw it roughly several times at first. Many things can go wrong. The letters you draw may not fit into the length available; you must then compress the actual letters, thereby spoiling the alphabet, or close the spacing, which may well ruin the appearance of the word. Obviously you can easily close up the straight vertical letters but this will leave others such as the round letters looking like great holes. It may be necessary, therefore, to reduce the height of the letters, but this may affect the balance of the whole panel. I think many of the pitfalls will be obvious – it is clear when two letters are too closely or widely spaced, but arriving at the finished plan can be a long and wearisome business, until you get the hang of it. Fortunately there are some excellent books on the subject and examples are everywhere to see. The width of the thick strokes is approximately one tenth of the height of the letter and the thin strokes half the width of the thick ones, but this again need not be rigidly adhered to.

Having completed the lettering on paper, plane a board of wood as smoothly as possible, oak is ideal, and trace the lettering onto it, the grain running horizontally along the line of the characters. Carving with the grain running vertically is considerably more difficult. Clamp the wood down onto a good solid bench top. If the bench top bounces every time you hit the chisel it is very disconcerting.

Take the vertical strokes first. Suppose the letters are 40mm ($1\frac{1}{2}''$) high. Take a sharp 35mm ($1\frac{1}{4}''$) firmer chisel and place the edge down the centre line of the stroke, held vertically; you may even go to the trouble of scoring the centre line with a try square and knife, as a guide. Strike the chisel firmly with the mallet driving it in about 3mm ($\frac{1}{8}''$) Fig. 130. This should stop 3mm ($\frac{1}{8}''$), short of the top and bottom of the letter, to allow for the serifs.

Now hold the chisel at an angle of about 55° with the cutting edge to the left-hand side of the stroke (Fig. 131). Strike it hard enough to cut to the bottom of the "V". Repeat this on the right-hand side of the letter (Fig. 132) and the chip should fall out, leaving a perfect v-shaped cut. If it doesn't, clean it up using hand pressure on the chisel.

This is the basic principle of incised letter carving, chip carving and most other carving. If you do not cut a clean chip, your carving

Fig. 130

Fig. 131

slightly to meet the vertical stroke we have just completed. It is clear that we have three different radii to deal with, and strictly speaking, only the external one is a true circle, the middle and inner ones being increasingly elliptical. Therefore, it follows that we must use three different sweeps of gouge.

First we find a gouge which fits the central line, and make a series of perpendicular cuts along it (Fig. 133, below).

Fig. 132

Fig. 133

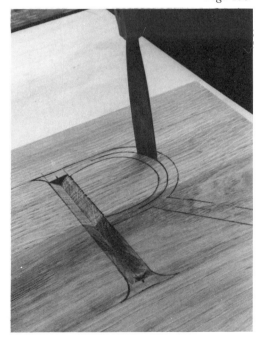

will always look untidy in the corners. It will also look unsightly if the first cut is too deep and shows at the bottom of the V.

Curved letters, without a doubt are more difficult. If we take the letter R as a typical case, let us consider the problems. The curved section is a semicircle, extended

Now select a gouge which fits the outer circumference and make a second series of cuts at 55° to incise the outer side of the V as in Fig. 134.

The inner cut is the most difficult since it requires a gouge that is slightly flatter than the curve of the inner edge of the letter. A perfectly fitting one invariably leaves slight ridges beween individual cuts and gives the curve a scalloped appearance. In some cases all or part of the inner curve can be best pared away with a small flat chisel, such as with the middle section of the R. Fig. 135.

We now come to the serifs. These are not

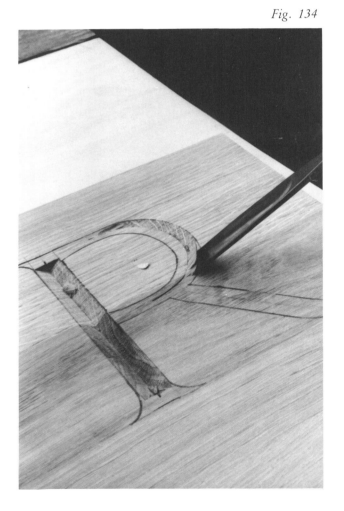

Fig. 134

Fig. 135

Fig. 136

Fig. 137

difficult to do, but difficult to do well, and they must be done well if the letters are to achieve the elegance and refinement that is their great appeal. Too often they end up as clumsy triangular chips attached to the top and bottom of the letters.

Taking the bottom of the vertical stroke of the R, we have before us the V-cut, terminating 3mm ($\frac{1}{8}$″) before the end of the stroke. Select a very sharp 9mm ($\frac{3}{8}$″) fishtail No. 3 gouge. The acute corners of the fishtail or spade gouge enable it to penetrate into the lowest corner of the serif. Starting with the left-hand serif as we are looking at it, upside down, place the cutting edge flat on the left-hand side of the V-cut, where it ends, the shaft parallel to the stroke, (Fig. 136). Now pushing the gouge forwards,

turning the handle slightly to the left and forcing the right-hand corner deeper into the wood, the cut should follow the line of the serif (Fig. 137).

Now repeat this, in reverse, on the right-hand serif. All that remains is to remove the chip by pushing the corner of the fishtail into the end of one serif, along the line of the bottom of the letter, at an angle of 55°, thus removing an inverted pyramid as in Fig. 138.

The point where the bottom of the V-cut meets the bottom of the serifs is always slightly deeper than the V-cut itself.

Where a thin stroke meets a thick one, or a serif, as at the middle and top of the R, always complete one stroke at a time so they run together naturally (Fig. 139).

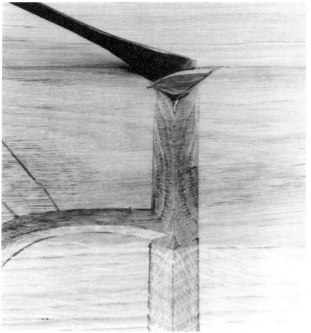

Fig. 138

Fig. 139

After some practice you will find it easier when carving a number of words to cut all the straight centre strokes first, then, having resharpened the chisel, make all the angled cuts. I think this makes for efficiency and more uniformity of angles and cuts. Strokes running along the grain can be troublesome and the vee tool can sometimes be used to advantage. I also usually nick the ends of these strokes to sever the fibres sufficiently to enable the chip to come out cleanly.

Having completed the lettering, rub the board down with fine abrasive paper and a block to remove pencil lines, etc. The finish is obviously determined by the end use of the work. For outside purposes I generally use oak, teak or iroko and finish with

oil, but inside, most timbers can be used, although highly figured wood can conflict with the legibility of the lettering.

Although there are people who use a vee tool for Roman lettering, I find it most unsatisfactory myself and would not recommend it. However, it can be used with excellent results for other types of lettering, in particular for imitating that written with a pen – italic, round-hand and other calligraphic styles – I sign all my work with a 3mm ($\frac{1}{8}''$) 45° vee tool in a typical round-hand used by the writing-masters of the nineteenth century. The example shown here is a 20th century adaptation of the round-hand using a pointed pen.

Inscribed lettering of this type with a vee tool is not difficult but requires considerable control over the tool in order to achieve a flowing line, and therefore a great deal of practice is necessary for the beginner. Also, it is very easy to overshoot the line and nigh impossible to correct. A soft, even cutting wood such as lime is excellent for this work; harder wood, such as oak, requires more pressure and therefore more control.

The writing is first drawn out very carefully indicating precisely the path of the two cutting edges (Fig. 140). With the tool at the peak of sharpness, make long sweeping cuts, avoiding, if possible, starting on a tight curve. Indicated, are the cuts I have made and their direction, but there is no hard and fast reason for them. I am left-handed and this may well affect my way of working. Fig. 141.

The vee tool method can also be used in conjunction with the normal incised method for typefaces such as "Old English", "Fraktur" and others.

Fig. 140

Fig. 141

RAISED LETTERING

There are many typefaces which cannot be cut by the incised method. Of course they could simply be cut into the wood as a flat bottomed channel, but they do not look very impressive. Incised Roman letters rely on the shadows cast for their effect whereas the shadows formed by the flat bottomed letters would have the opposite effect. These letters then, basically ones without serifs, are carved as raised lettering. Bauhaus is the basis of many of these typefaces. In the aftermath of the industrial revolution two reactions made themselves known. In Britain, William Morris and his followers reacted strongly against machine-made products and reintroduced hand craftsmanship. The movement persisted for a long time, perhaps even to the present, but its products were very expensive and some people would say anachronistic. Morris's influence is still very strong in virtually all fields of art and design.

The opposite reaction came from Germany where the Bauhaus was set up by a group of artists and designers; the Bauhaus took the machine age to its heart and tried to eliminate handcraft. Its influence is also still strongly felt in many fields, particularly printing. Letters without serifs were introduced by printers to whom they caused considerable problems. These typefaces were thought so ugly they became known as "grotesques". The problems of letter spacing and word spacing still existed though. The Bauhaus eliminated this by creating a typeface that is mathematically constructed. The thickness of the stroke is always the same, and the letter space is also the same thickness as the letters. All letters are constructed from straight lines and circles. Fig. 142.

In the sample shown the unit of thickness is 10mm (the width of the strokes). The "b" is constructed from a vertical stroke and two circles joined together. The tail of the letter rises 10mm above the upper circle. The "a" is formed by two circles, the lower one 5mm left of the upper one, connected by straight strokes. The spaces between are 10mm. The circles are 10mm inside diameter and 30mm outside diameter. These letters despite their mathematical basis require very careful drawing.

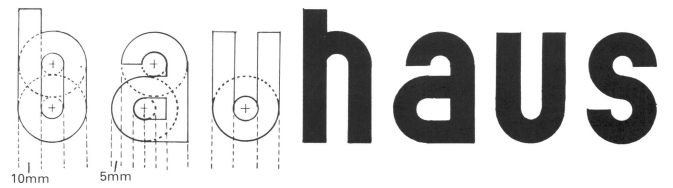

10mm   5mm

Fig. 142 Straight lines and circles are the combinations used in the build up of the letters, and this combined with the rigid adherence to the thickness of the individual sections gives the rather bland symmetrical appearance.

To turn this theory into practical exercise first draw out the design and then trace onto the wood with carbon paper (Fig. 143). Any raised edge or frame is also drawn on. Raised lettering is not usually very deeply cut, in this case 7 or 8mm ($^5/_{16}''$) and the sides are not perpendicular but slope outward a couple of degrees. The quickest way to recess the background is with an electric router. This ensures a perfectly flat even background and skilled hands bring the cutter very close to the letters (Fig. 144). However, when an electric router makes a mistake, it makes a bad one.

Fig. 143

Fig. 144

Alternatively, this waste can be removed with gouges and chisels. In this sample virtually all of it can be taken out with a 6mm ($\frac{1}{4}''$) No. 9 cut down to a millimetre or so of the finished level as in Fig. 145.

The letters must now have their final shape cut and this requires very sharp tools and clean cutting. Using a gouge somewhat flatter than the outside curves, say 12mm ($\frac{1}{2}''$) No. 3, using the inside of the cutting edge, pare away the waste around the curved section. Remember to slope them outwards (Fig. 146).

Fig. 145

Fig. 146

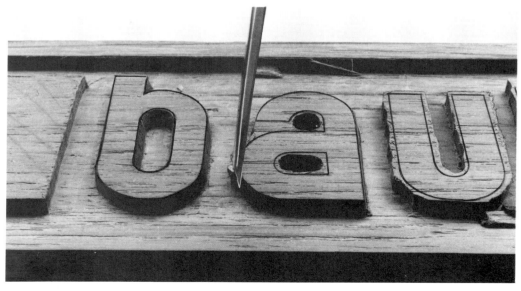

Now using flat chisels cut the straight sections (Fig. 147). This is all simple enough, but needs to be right first time. The curves inside the loops of the letters are slightly more difficult. Use a gouge that has a smaller curvature than the letter and pare away the waste, sloping in towards the centre of the opening. At all times great care must be taken not to cut too deeply as this will leave chisel cuts in the finished background round the edges of the letters and look most unsightly. Having finished the shaping of the letters the background must be cleaned up. This requires a grounding tool – a spoon

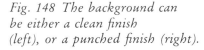

Fig. 147

Fig. 148 The background can be either a clean finish (left), or a punched finish (right).

bent flat chisel about 3–6mm (1–$\frac{1}{4}$″) wide, to clean round the edge of the letter. The larger areas are easier to do with a spoon bent No. 2 or 3, which will leave a very slightly tooled finish.

Sometimes the background of lettering is punched using the matting punches available from carving tool suppliers, or by making your own. This pitted surface tends to throw the lettering out more and can look quite impressive if carefully done. However, it has in the past been associated with inferior carving on cheap furniture and this has given rise to an aversion to the use of a punched background. Fig. 148.

Shown below are some examples of the different approaches to letter carving. (Fig. 149).

G and H are probably the easiest, being formed by merely cutting the outline of the letter with chisels or a knife and in the first case, punching the background, and in the second, punching the letter itself, thus making it legible merely by changing the texture.

Fig. 149

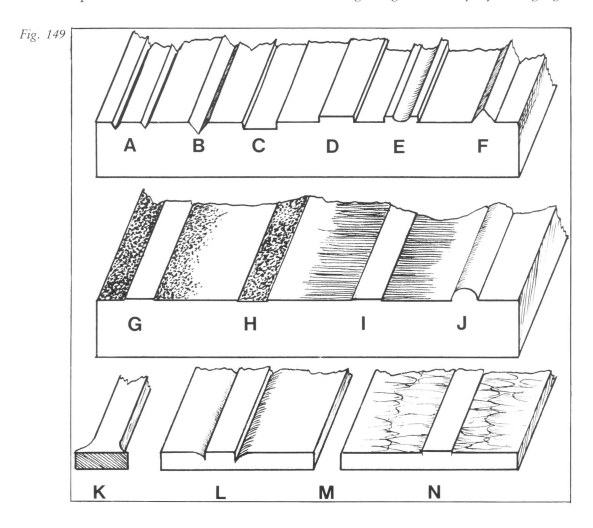

"I" is similar but the background is textured with parallel lines made with a vee tool or small gouge. In the case of "N" the area round the letter is tooled with a gouge to create the difference.

"L" is almost as simple as these, the outline of the letter being deeply cut with chisels and gouges and the area outside it rounded off to give a cushioned effect. "A" consists merely of outlining the letter with a vee tool or small gouge. "B" is standard incised carving, "C" is a recessed channel, and "D" raised lettering as just described. This is sometimes decorated in other ways, such as having a groove cut in the centre, as in "E". "F". and "J" combine the difficulties of raised lettering with the added problems of shaping the letter into a "V" or semi-circle. "K" is a completely cut out letter, which could be subsequently carved, and "M" a fretted letter.

SOURCES OF INSPIRATION

If you take time out to look for examples of the effective and imaginative use of carved lettering in wood what soon becomes apparent is the great scarcity of it, although there is an abundance of the basic incised Roman, usually of indifferent quality. A visit to the nearest church should show you a few examples of memorial inscriptions, name boards and bible quotations. Coats of arms invariably have a motto carved on a scroll under the shield, but these are usually of stone. Of course what can be carved in stone can be carved in wood and a look round a cemetery might be rewarding. The first example I found was on a small German panel I happened to own which has "Fruhling" (Spring) daintily carved in raised script on a ribbon. Made in pear, the work is very fine and appropriate for the subject (Fig. 150).

Fig. 150

The monogram is an art of its own and whole books are devoted to it. I find the one illustrated in Fig 151 rather confused. Carved on the back of a mahogany chair, it stands for Regimental Sergeant Major Pioneer Corps, and a brass coat of arms was fixed to the rear. The background is punched and the whole piece is badly worn. The second monogram shown in Fig. 152 is much clearer and of a higher quality. It is a modern lectern from a church, carved in parana pine with the letters in gilt. The raised gothic lettering (Fig. 153) from the same church is excellent workmanship although the background punching is coarse and irregular. This type of raised letter requires most painstaking and meticulous work, but is very decorative on furniture and fittings.

Fig. 151

Fig. 152

Fig. 153

Fig. 154

Another example of the decorative use of lettering can be seen on the gateway shown in Fig. 154. This large structure is the entrance to a cemetery and is a memorial to a dead naval officer. The long rows of letters along the oak beam are far more enlightening visually than the quotation is spiritually, making what would be a heavy dark build-ing, lighter and far more interesting. The date is 1914, where there would normally be a piece of carved foliage, is a clever contrivance but superbly executed in an elaborate ornate letter form. Notice the moulding appearing to run under the number and Tudor rose – very clever stuff.

Polyphons (Fig. 155) were large musical boxes, made around the turn of the century, which invariably have their name cut into them somewhere. The letter form is basically the same as Roman to carve but perhaps slightly more difficult. On the machines it is normally painted gold.

Fig. 155

Fig. 156

Standing cups from the Jacobean period are beautiful things, and I think much of their interest comes from the delicate lacey design and lettering that cover the surfaces (Fig. 156). I'm not sure whether this is painted, burnt or carved on, but it is very shallow, fine and small.

Finally, in the decorative vein, my own contribution is a sign for my studio door carved with a vee tool in about an hour (Fig 157). Being about 250mm (10″) in diameter, it is really too small. The small curves are too tight for the vee tool to cope with smoothly and it tends to crush the wood on the outside edge. However, having drawn it on the wood accurately it is almost as easy as writing.

House signs are a lucrative occupation and I have selected four which show a range of styles. The first (Fig 158) has a starkness which belies the pretty name and the pretty house it belongs to. Chopped into a board of yew one can discern the heavy toolcuts at the bottom of the letters. Bramble Cottage (Fig. 159) is a very slick piece of lettering, lots of curves cleanly cut and look at the perfect likeness of the A's and E's. The style is attractive without being 'twee' and very easy to read. April Cottage (Fig. 160) is made from cut out letters fixed to the backboard and very effective it is, if perhaps inappropriate for an ancient stone cottage. The letters must be fairly simple to cut on a good fretsaw, but by hand I think they would take as long as carving.

Amesbury (Fig. 161) looks to me as though it may well have been done on a machine. All the round serifs and rounded looking corners, the immaculate precision of the cutting gives that impression. However, there is nothing on it to indicate the use of a machine or chisel. Notice the bad spacing the of "A" and the "Y". To balance these large spaces the whole word should have been spread out equally.

Fig. 158

Fig. 159

Fig. 160

Fig. 161

The easy way out for the DIY man – a table lamp built entirely of old wooden printers' blocks (Fig. 162). These were sold nationally through department stores and the mellow stained wood looks very striking. There was until recently a printer in Gloucester, who covered an entire wall in the reception office with them. Although these letters were made in thousands on machines, the idea of using the alphabet as an abstract decorative shape is a sound one.

Fig. 163 shows a Victorian relief carving, naive in style but technically quite competent. It is painted, although the paint is very blackened and corroded. The raised lettering is simple and matter of fact but very nicely carved and certainly makes the panel more interesting, but more importantly, it explains immediately and obviously what the subject is about.

Fig. 164 is taken from the lid of a padauk jewellery box, made in the Far East. Everything on it is typically Chinese except for the monogram which is very much of Victorian England. As with most oriental carving it is technically superb, the letters being about 12mm ($\frac{1}{2}''$) deep. It was presumably commissioned by some English visitor in the 19th century.

The lettering shown in Fig. 165 is unusual in being set into the hollow curve of a moulding about 100mm (4″) wide. It is not cut from the solid but has been cut, presumably from another matching curved length of oak and fixed in place.

Fig. 162

Fig. 163

Fig. 164

Fig. 165

Fig. 166

Fig. 167

Fig. 168

Another sample from a church, Fig. 166, shows a beautiful piece of lettering carved in solid oak with a continuous folded scroll as a background. The alphabet is, I think, particularly pleasant and the hollowing of the surface is very effective. Notice that the restriction on the spacing caused by the equal lengths allowed for each panel have caused the "S" and "E" to be too close, and a hole to appear between the "L" and "S".

The large initials in Fig. 167 are at least 300mm (12″) high, and carved into the top of a large oak church door at Winchcombe in Gloucestershire. As can be seen, the bottom part of the letters has been fretted out on the front side of the groove which holds the panel. Unfortunately the "K" has been broken. This is woodcarving at its best and an excellent use of lettering both as decoration and as a memorial, in this case to a former bishop.

Fig. 168 is a simple and beautiful house name. The technique is excellent, the typeface ideal and the spacing almost perfect. There is perhaps slightly too much space between the "T" and "h".

Fig. 169 shows two Japanese name stamps about 100mm (4″) long and carved in a very hard wood (perhaps ebony). Technically excellent, they were, I believe, inked and stamped on paper or silk. Wood block printing is, of course, basically carried out with a type of relief carving and may well provide some ideas for further experiment.

Fig. 169

Fig. 170 is an example of a carving of my own where I have used lettering all around the edge of the base. This not only adds content to the subject of the piece, "Merlin", since it is an incantation in latin for raising the Devil, but also acts as a bridge between the carving and the mahogany plinth. I have also used monograms of the year and my initials on the table legs. Fig. 171

Fig. 171

Fig. 170

EXAMPLES OF CARVED LETTERING

BOWL

I bought this olive wood bowl for a few pounds including the servers, feeling that its plainness begged to be embellished. Being, unable to think of some apt phrase which would give new significance to a tossed salad I decided on the line from *Macbeth*. The lettering is Celtic, taken from the *Lindsfarne Gospels*, in a particularly beautifully written hand.

The bowl being 76mm (30″) round and the words consisting of 28 letters including spaces, it was pretty easy to decide on 25mm (1″) high letters, averaging 25mm (1″) wide, leaving 62mm (2½″) of empty space to divide the end from the beginning. The lettering was then drawn onto a strip of paper and traced onto the bowl. Fig. 172 and 173.

In work such as this you can generally hold the bowl in the vice so that the letters can be comfortably carved. I used a vee tool for the thin lines and the long tapering ends. Most of the heavier lines are best done with a round nosed, flat gouge, the ends being finished with a small, flat fishtail. The decorative bird's heads, etc., are done with a 2mm vee tool. (Fig. 174, finished bowl.)

Fig. 172

Fig. 173

Fig. 174

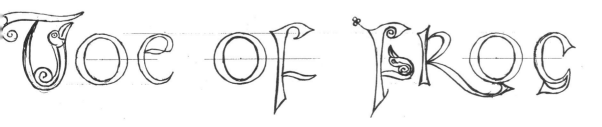

INCISED GOTHIC

Like many types of lettering that are written with a pen the German and Old English characters are not entirely suitable for incising, but can be done quite satisfactorily. The ends of the straight strokes require neatly cutting into inverted pyramids or flat ended vees. Fig. 175. The thin straight strokes are chipped in with a flat chisel No. 1. The variable, irregular curves are also quite difficult and really require a couple of shallow gouges ground to a thumbnail profile which can be slid round the bends. The finished article is quite impressive, even if difficult to read. Fig. 176.

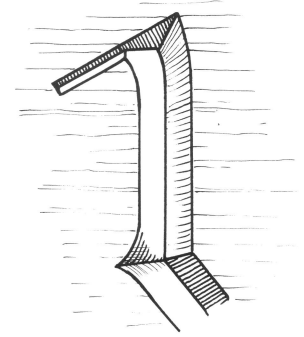

Fig. 175

Fig. 176

CUPRINOL

This panel, commissioned by an advertising agency, presented the opportunity to do something a little unusual, not for a flight of fancy but for hard, commercial reason. The basic artwork was presented to me (Fig. 177) by the agency and it was decided that it should be on an oak panel with a frame of the same material.

The heavy block lettering is raised and the middle section incised, giving a variety of levels which makes the piece more interesting. A router is ideal to reduce the

Fig. 177

Fig. 178

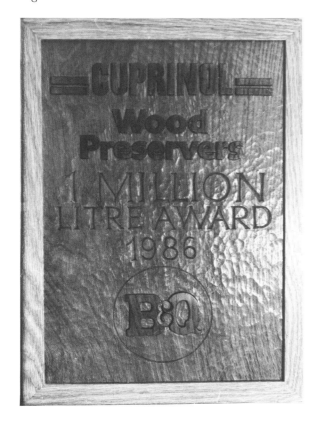

background on a panel of this type and with careful handling only the minimum of work with a chisel is needed to complete the raised letters. Notice that the grain of the wood is running from top to bottom which makes incised letters slightly more difficult but is sometimes inevitable. Fig. 178.

RUSSIAN SHIELD

Fig. 180. This Russian lettering was for an Englishman whose Russian wife was, for a time, unable to leave the Soviet Union. The idea of the shield is quite pleasant, although it may be the novelty of the Cyrillic characters which gives it charm.

I was given the artwork on paper to be carved actual size, so I took the opportunity to photostat the original and, using the copy, taped it to the wood and cut through the paper lightly with chisels thus outlining the letters with complete accuracy onto the wood (Fig. 179). The background was then routed and the cutting of the letters completed. I punched the background, leaving a small border, and gave it a wax finish.

Fig. 179

Fig. 180 (By courtesy of Mr. and Mrs J. Nation)

MARILLION

Fig. 182. This lettering was exceedingly difficult to carve, at least on the scale I did it. It proved to me that some types of lettering are not suitable for carving in the solid. The outside edges can be routed (Fig. 181) and cleaned up with chisels and gouges, but the tiny irregular shaped holes in the letters, in this case 19mm ($\frac{3}{4}''$) deep, proved arduous to do cleanly, without, at the same time, damaging the top edges. I sanded the top heavily when the cutting was finished, then chamfered the lower edges in an attempt to imitate the original on the record sleeve. This does not really work. Were I doing this again I would have carefully cut away the block of wood where the letter was to

be. This could be done quite easily leaving a strip about 9mm ($\frac{3}{8}''$) intact. This could be planed up into a small flat panel, the grain exactly in its original position on the carving. The lettering could then be cut from this panel on a fretsaw and the appropriate edges chamfered. Alternatively, the panel could be planed to about 3mm ($\frac{1}{8}''$) thick, or even thinner, and another panel of light wood, say, sycamore, made. Then the dark part of the lettering could be fretted from the walnut and the light part (that is the dark area plus the light edges) fretted from the sycamore. With these two glued together, the letters could be glued onto small 6mm ($\frac{1}{4}''$) pegs so that they "floated" just above the surface of the sky. I think this would look quite impressive.

Fig. 181

Fig. 182

CHAPTER SEVEN

Alphabets and Monograms

There are hundreds of alphabets and these can be found in specialised books or in the catalogues of the companies that make transfer letters. I have included some of the more classic and traditional ones and a few more modern ones. A little study will show that some, such as Romantiques and Normandes, would be very difficult to do effectively by any means, whilst others lend themselves to incising, outlining, raising, fretting, etc. Observation of lettering in the environment will reveal more bad examples than good, some from organisations that should know better.

Monograms are a fascinating study and have aroused almost scientific interest in the past when magical properties were attributed to them. Some monograms have become very well known such as those of the artists Lautrec and Durer. Since most woodcarvers will want to sign their work they might well use a monogram as I do myself.

Alphabets illustrated on pp 127 to 149
Monographs illustrated on pp 150 to 155

Caslon

abcdefghijk

lmnopqrfst

uvwxyz

1234567890

ABCDEF

GHIJKLM

NOPQRS

TUVWXYZ

Garamond italic

ABCDEFGHIJKL
MNOPQRST
UVWXYZ
abcdefghijklmnopqr
ſstuvvwxyzææ
12345&67890

Baskerville

ABCDEFGHI
JKLMNO
PQRSTUVW
XYZ

abcdefghjkmn
opqrstuvwxyz
12345&67890

RWL-I

OPTIMA

ABCDEFGHI
JKLMNOPQRSTU
VWXYZ

abcdefghijklmno
pqrstuvwxyz
12345 & 67890

OLD FACE OPEN

ABCD
EFGHIJKLMNO
PQRSTUVW
XYZ
1234567890

WEISS

ABCDEF
GHIJKLMN
OPQRST
UVWXYZ

WEISS

ABCDEE

FGHIJKLMN

OPQRSTU

VWXYZ

Firmin Didot

ABCDEFGHIJ
KLMNOPQRS
TUVWXYZ
abcdefghijklmno
pqrstuvwxyz
1234567890

Gill Sans

ABCDEFHIJ
KLMNOPQR
TUVWXYZ
1234567890
abcdefghi
jklmnopqrstu
vwxyz&

EGYPTIENNES GRASSES (Bold Egyptian)

ABCDEFG
HIJKLMNOP
QRSTUVW
XYZ
abcdefghijk
lmnopqrstu
vwxyz
1234567890

Gras Vibert

ABCDEFGHI
JKLMNOPQ
RSTUWXYZ

abcdefghijklmn
opqrstuvwxyz

1234567890

Walbaum-Fraktur

𝕬 𝕭 𝕮 𝕯 𝕰 𝕱 𝕲 𝕳 𝕴

𝕶 𝕷 𝕸 𝕹 𝕺 𝕻 𝕼 𝕽 𝕾 𝕿 𝖀

𝖁 𝖂 𝖃 𝖄 𝖅

a b c d e f g h i j k l m n o p q

r ſ s t u v w x y z ä ö ü

1 2 3 4 5 6 7 8 9 0

ANTIQUES SERRÉES GRASSES
(Bold Condensed Sans Serif)

ABCDEFGHIJ
KLMNOPQRSTU
VWXYZ

abcdefghijkl
mnopqrstuvwxyz

1234567890

ECRITURE ITALIENNE.

A B C D E

F G H I J K

L M N

O P Q R S T U

V W X Y Z &c

abcdefghijklmnopqrstuvwxyzz

SPANISH ITALIC (c. 1776)

ROMANTIQUES

A B C D E F
G H I J K L M
N O P Q R S T
U V W X Y Z
1 2 3 4 5 6 7 8 9 0

NORMANDES

ABCDE

FGHIJK

LMNO

PQRSTU

VWXYZ

12&34

567890

ROTUNDA (c. 1553)

𝔄 𝔅 ℭ 𝔇 𝔈 𝔉
𝔊 𝔥 𝔍 𝔎 𝔏 𝔐
𝔐 𝔒 𝔓 𝔔 𝔕 𝔖
𝔗 𝔘 𝔚 𝔛 𝔜 𝔷

a b c d e f g
h i k l m n o
p q r 2 ſ s t
v u w x y z

Ancient Black

ABCDEFGH

abcdefghijklmnopq

JKLMNOPQ

rfstuvwxyz

RSTUWXYZ

UNCIAL

FESTIS · APR̄BISAUTĒ
MINIMEDICITUR · NISI
SOLOINPASCHA · QUAN
DOUEROLAETANIAAGI
TURNEQUEGLORIAIN
EXCELSISDONEQUEALL
CANITUR POSTMODŪ
DICITURORATIO · DEIN
DESEQUITURAPOSTO
LUS ITEMGRADALIS
SIUEALLELUIA POST
MODUMLEGITUREU
ANGELIUMDEINDEOF
FERTORIŪETDICITUR
ORATIOSUPEROBLATA
QUACŌPLETADICIT SACER
DOSEXCELSAUOCE ·

ORNAMENTAL TITLE PAGE (c. 1496)

ORNAMENTAL TEXTUR MINUSCULES (c. 1545)

ORNAMENTAL TEXTUR MINUSCULES (c. 1545)

AA · AA · AA

AA · AA · AA

·VARIOUS·TREATMENTS·OF·THE·SAME·DESIGN·

AA   AA   AB

BA   AAB   BBA

AC   CA   AAC

PPA   AQ   QA

AR   RA   AAR

RRA   AS   SA

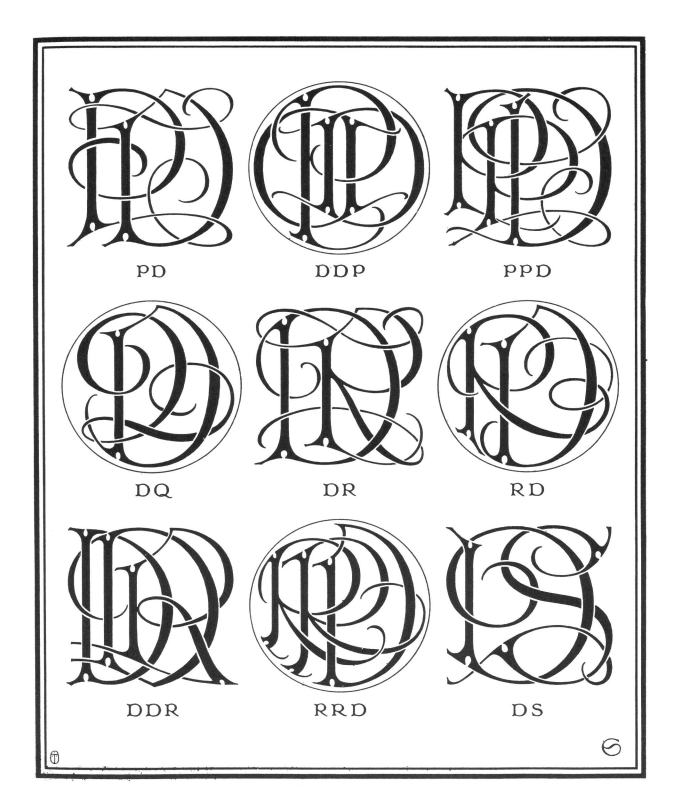

PD   DDP   PPD

DQ   DR   RD

DDR   RRD   DS

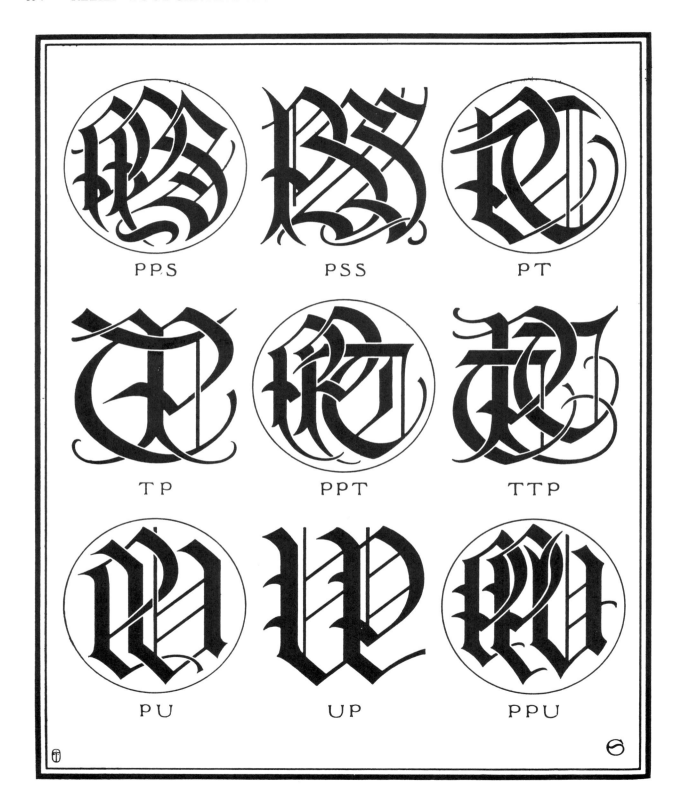

PPS   PSS   PT

TP   PPT   TTP

PU   UP   PPU

KKV   KW   WK

KKW   WWK   KX

KY   KZ   ZK

Index